SPEAKING FRANKLY

SPEAKING FRANKLY

A Southern Boy's Journey from
Slaughterhouse to Creation of the
World's Top Hot dog Brand

Clyde Riley
with Doron Levin

To order additional copies of this book, contact:
Xlibris LLC
1-888-795-4274
www.Xlibris.com
Orders@Xlibris.com
550027

DEDICATION

I dedicate this book to my loving wife, Helen Riley.

CONTENTS

FOREWORD

Why I'm Writing This Book

I was sixty-five years old in June 1992 and had arrived at my retirement as the president of Hygrade Food Products Corporation, the Detroit-based meatpacking company that had employed me for nearly half a century. The time had come to look back and reflect on the meaningful and prosperous life I've lived, to recall the places I'd visited and sights I'd seen, to remember and thank my friends, family, and colleagues, to count my blessings, and finally, to explore and ponder the reasons why my career as a businessman had turned out so rewarding and fulfilling.

This is my story.

Very little of what happened to me early in life hinted at how events would unfold. My prospects as a youngster growing up as the son of a sharecropper in Alabama during the depths of the Depression certainly didn't suggest I was headed for a business career packed with travel, adventure, and dealings with colorful figures from all walks of life. In those days, if you were born on a farm in rural Alabama that's likely where you stayed. There's nothing shameful about that. In fact, I'm exceptionally proud of my background, family, neighbors, and heritage, as well as the place where I grew up.

Farming was a rugged, satisfying, and honorable way for my family to live and support itself. In retrospect, perhaps, rural life looks much harder today than it did then. Only by today's standards may it be said that we had little in the way of material comfort. I never felt poor or deprived as a child, probably because none of the other farming families had very much either. Comforts and technological advances were becoming common in cities. But we rarely saw them unless we were visiting in Montgomery, a town I had the chance to see exactly once in my youth. As unimaginable as it might seem in this day of iPads and smartphones, I didn't have the experience of talking on a telephone until I was eighteen, when I answered the phone at work for the first time. For some strange reason, the number of that phone sticks in my mind.

My parents were of modest means. They were very proud people and had reason to be: they toiled hard for what they possessed and earned their way in the world. Our family resided in a small, simple wood-framed house with four or five rooms in a town called Slocomb, not far from Dothan, about ten miles from Alabama's border with Florida. We had no electricity, no telephone, no indoor plumbing, and very few possessions. We drew our water from a well with a rope and bucket. As a young child, I had one pair of shoes, a shirt and trousers, a raincoat, and a pair of goggles. My father presented me with the goggles so I could see during rainy days on my two-and-a-half-mile walk to Malvern school. My mother sewed my underwear and other clothing from discarded cloth flour sacks. Toys were scarce. I do recall owning a cap pistol, a prop used in games of cowboys and Indians.

Looking back on my childhood, I suppose it was destined that someday I would leave that way of life. Though I was a farm boy through and through, I amazingly managed never to learn how to milk our only cow. I was more interested in my studies at school, which was fine with my parents. Farming didn't interest me, as it did my older brother. He worked with our dad all over the forty acres we leased and, later, on the small farm we inherited from my mother's father. Wilburn, my brother, had quit school in seventh grade to help. He took quickly to the many skills and chores inherent in running a farm. Since he was eight years older than me, I regarded him more as an adult than as a sibling.

My father, Monroe Riley, rose daily at 4:00 a.m. to feed and tend the livestock and then was gone all day in the fields. I grew up in a world where discipline, frugality, and self-reliance were essential if you hoped to survive the uncertainties of weather, disease, accidents, and poor crop prices. Undoubtedly, the conditions under which we lived shaped my character and beliefs and made me grateful for all the blessings I would receive.

My mother, Ada, was born in 1884. She was the most powerful influence on me, followed by a couple of my teachers. She taught me my ABCs and how to count to a hundred before I started school. She was an extremely capable woman who, had she been alive today, would have been able to do anything she wanted.

I was the first member of my immediate family to finish the eighth grade and then became the first to graduate from high school. It was my good luck that my parents, both of whom only benefitted from third-grade educations, wanted me to be successful at school and always made sure I could attend classes and had time to complete my homework. When the rest of my family was preparing peanut seeds for the following year's crop, I was completing my English and math assignments.

I was a "mama's boy," sheltered from the more difficult and arduous tasks of farming. Because my parents and brother shouldered most of the duties on the farm, mine always were few and simple. During harvest season an extra set of hands always was welcome. Sometimes in the late afternoon when the sun began to set, my mother and I would pick cotton together. That memory remains very vivid and dear to me because of the time I spent with her.

Unlike most boys my age, I found sports to be uninteresting. I was drawn instead to my lessons at school, especially in math and science, and addressed homework assignments with gusto. The result was excellent grades and glowing approval from my teachers. School provided me knowledge about the world beyond Slocomb; the homework and tests demonstrated to me at an early age that meticulous preparation was vital for anything worth accomplishing.

I loved when my parents gave me little jobs or projects around the house, to fix a loose board or clean up the barn. I relished the challenge of being responsible to complete a task. I savored the feeling of accomplishment. By the time I was a teenager, my duties were generating a bit of pocket money, allowing me to pay for my own treats, to go to the movies in town, drink a milkshake, and buy a book or magazine. I especially enjoyed a series called Big Little Books, as well as western adventures and comic books featuring Dick Tracy and Superman. Money per se didn't occupy my thoughts. Years later, the day I got my first real job after high school, my dad asked me how much I would be paid. Sheepishly, I admitted to him that I'd forgotten to ask.

The rural South, of course, was distinctive and much different than the North, operating according to a characteristic code of speech and behavior. Folks were taught manners at home and made a point of minding them. You had to be careful when you chose your words and to avoid vulgarity or profanity in public, lest someone take offense. By the standards of today, farming society in the South was polite and modest, perhaps a touch prudish. For example, I never heard the word "pregnant" in mixed company until I was an adult, and that first time shocked me. Southerners preferred the euphemism "in a family way." As a youngster brought up on a farm, I understood the concept of sexuality and reproduction; yet I was quite innocent: women and men wore loose-fitting work clothes most of the time such that I didn't pay much attention until I attended high school how differently their bodies were shaped.

Segregation of the races was the law and custom, especially in rural areas and small towns. Blacks weren't considered the social or legal equals of whites. Black and white children didn't study in the same schools, eat at the same lunch counters, or drink at the same fountains. Three decades before the civil rights movement, I never saw or heard anyone question the separation of the races, so I didn't either. By the same token, I never heard any hateful or bigoted speech at home. A black family lived on the same property as our house; the man of the house worked for my dad for a daily wage. The children went to a different school than I did; we didn't play together.

I grew up as a painfully shy and introverted child. When guests came to our home, I often hid in the barn. But I was aware, always watching and listening, peeking from behind the corner, sizing up who and what I was seeing. I got pretty good at it. After a few minutes of listening to someone speak, I believed I knew if a person was an optimist or a pessimist, insecure or self-confident, modest or conceited. And by apprehending a person's attitude, often I could guess what they might say or how they might approach a situation or task.

I had never heard of Pearl Harbor until the day after that Sunday morning in 1941, when I was fifteen and in the tenth grade. We didn't yet own a radio so had no idea until the next day at school, when the attack was all everyone was discussing. Once the war had begun, all of us boys who would be graduating from Slocomb high school in 1944 realized we'd probably be drafted.

Because I wasn't yet eighteen at my graduation, several months remained before my reporting date to the military, providing me with time to work. As men left for war, the opportunities were plentiful. My first job was at a meatpacking plant, the biggest private employer in Dothan. The slaughterhouse's parent company was located in Indianapolis, having expanded to the U.S. from Ireland in the nineteenth century. I was assigned to weigh hogs at a rate of forty cents an hour, the federal minimum wage. In August 1945, I reported for my induction into the U.S. Navy.

My stint in the navy had a transformative impact on me, though it had nothing to do with combat. My service lasted only nine months, coming to an end a short time after World War II had ended. I returned home a different person. The slaughterhouse rehired me, this time as a clerk. I was responsible for collecting facts and figures from the plant and conveying them to the office. Meatpacking was an industry that required the great majority of its workers to expend physical effort in the course of turning live animals into food. During the next half of a century, working at many plants and in many offices, my jobs required intelligence, energy, and a positive outlook, which I was fortunate to possess in abundance.

My business career took me from the South to the Midwest and finally to the Detroit area. I married a wonderful woman, Patricia Joann Thomas. We raised two beautiful children, Margaret and David, and enjoyed many happy times together before illness brought Pat's life to an early end. But life wasn't through providing me with blessings or happiness. I would find love again.

Today young people leave home for college or go into business, planning how to climb the ladder, maybe dreaming of being the president of a company or starting an enterprise. That wasn't my experience. We worked because we had to support ourselves. I never expected too much, never looked too far ahead, and dreamed very little. Instead, I concentrated on performing the tasks assigned to me as well as possible and tried to absorb everything I could about what went on around me. In fifty years of employment, every job was important to me, no matter how large or small.

After my first series of clerical jobs, I was asked to learn about sales and marketing. Having gained a bit of knowledge and skill in those disciplines, I was promoted to the managerial ranks, eventually rising to the executive level and, finally, to the presidency. I filled gaps in my knowledge by attending school at night. Plain old good luck was in my favor. A determined attitude to perform in exemplary fashion, no matter the assignment, helped immensely too. Later on, moving into leadership roles, I was able to attract talented individuals and, especially at important moments, motivate them to perform. The rewards were many. The money was good, of course, much more than a farm boy ever thought possible.

More than the material benefits, I valued the places I was able to travel, the people I met, and of course, the tremendous satisfaction of experiencing the adventures of business and prevailing in just about every mission or task I attempted.

In the meatpacking industry, many of the executives I knew or met had hopped from job to job among several companies during their careers, rising in pay and responsibility. I'm especially proud that I made it to the top of Hygrade by staying with one company. Its name and owners changed a few times. My original employer was bought by a financially stronger company—and again by an even stronger one. Along the way, as good luck and timing would have it, I was at the controls when my company was creating a good name in the food business to become one of the world's most valuable and memorable brands, Ball Park Franks.

I wrote this book to share my remarkable journey with others: friends, family, and coworkers, as well as with readers who may be interested in the food industry, branding, marketing, a slice of twentieth-century history, and one man's passage from Southern farm to factory floor to corporate suite.

The changes in my industry and the economy have been striking, and they continue unabated. Corporations have altered their methods of operating and continue to do so. A few important principles, however, have remained constant. First and foremost is the vast opportunity that exists and endures for anyone who is a motivated, energetic individual to make a mark in American business and society.

Though my story differs from others in its specifics, I'm hardly the first or last person from a humble background—without financial resources, connections, or the advantage of a college diploma—to rise to the top of a company, industry, or profession. We Americans aren't as class-conscious or as rigid as most other cultures in the world. The United States is full of prospects and loaded with openings and pathways for those with energy and a positive attitude; that's why immigrants from all over the world are waiting in long lines to become citizens.

My parents refused to accept government "relief," as it was called during the Great Depression. When I think back to the difficulties they overcame with grit and determination, I feel very proud. I would be proud to accept a job at McDonald's today rather than to live from unemployment compensation or food stamps.

I hope that young people who read my story will be inspired to set goals, to apply for jobs, to seek knowledge, to prepare, and to propose new solutions for old problems. No one should limit himself or herself or be overly impressed by what has been created before. Lots of my time and effort was devoted to an ordinary, relatively uncelebrated food, the hot dog. One might conclude that hot dogs have been thoroughly exhausted, from the standpoint of innovation. Nonsense. A tastier, better hot dog, packaged more creatively and served in a manner no one anticipated, is waiting to be invented. A more creative marketing campaign is waiting to be conjured. A better way of doing just about anything is always around the corner.

CHAPTER 1

Life in a Small Alabama Farm Town

I was born at home in Slocomb, Alabama, on October 16, 1926. Hospitals and doctors were scarce. They also were expensive. Few women living on farms gave birth in hospitals in those days; instead, they relied on midwives. My mother, Ada Riley, had lost three babies in childbirth. She had been warned against having any more children after my older brother. We were fortunate with her last pregnancy, which resulted in my birth.

My mother's parents, David and Amanda May, resided in Geneva, about fifteen miles southwest of Slocomb. My grandmother's ancestry was Dutch, my grandfather's was English. My grandmother ran a boardinghouse, and my grandfather worked as a drayman, delivering all kinds of goods by horse-drawn wagon. A very early memory is of him taking me to see a water-powered gristmill, where grain was turned into meal. Later on, the Mays bought a farm in Slocomb. My father met my mother in the course of working as a day laborer on my grandparents' farm.

My father's father, George Riley, was a farmer. His wife, Elizabeth, came from a family named Forrester, which owned a prosperous ice cream business. On both sides of my family I'd have to say the women were the stronger and more capable partners in the marriage, a tendency that repeated itself in my parents' generation.

My father, Monroe Riley, was a sharecropper. That meant we lived on and tended land that belonged to someone else and paid a portion of our harvest as rent. We grew corn, peanuts, and cotton on a forty-acre tract. Some of it went to feed chickens, hogs, and chickens, the rest sold to provide us cash. The owner of the land also owned our simple, wooden house and provided a mule. We kept a half share of whatever we could sell, the other half belonging to the landlord.

The crash of 1929 wiped out my father's meager financial holdings. Luckily, a year later my mother's family invited us to come live with them and take over the operation of their sixty-acre farm near Slocomb. Her parents had reached an age that made it difficult to run their farm. This move marked a big jump in our earning and financial security. We grew cash crops, including peanuts and cotton, and raised hogs. My grandparents were in their seventies when we came to live with them, quite a ripe old age in the 1930s, and within a few years they both passed away.

Moving to my grandparents' farm was an important event, because it provided our family stability. Typically, sharecroppers moved from farm to farm, rarely making friends or having relationships with neighbors or schoolmates. My life would have been more difficult if we had had to move every year. Once we took over my grandparents' farm, our neighbors and my schoolmates remained more or less the same until I left home.

My childhood was very happy. We were a typical farming family, very grateful and content with what we had, which was very little by today's terms. My friends and I played games, ran across the wide expanse of open land, and engaged in activities that we thought were enjoyable, though they would have been regarded as dangerous or irresponsible in today's safety-conscious society. Every house kept firearms, and we boys were taught how to shoot. I learned how to handle a .22-caliber rifle and a 12-gauge shotgun. We played on the railroad tracks. We jumped out of trees and swam in water holes. There was little money for toys or board games. My family's only two big purchases that I can recall from my childhood were mainly for my benefit: a bicycle and a battery-powered radio. The radio required an antenna, so my dad and I cut down two small trees and constructed one.

By the time I was a teenager, the nation's entry in World War II was looking more and more likely. Following the Japanese attack on Pearl Harbor in 1941, our high school history teacher warned us to be prepared, because the boys were sure to be drafted. In fact, young men from our area had been volunteering for duty prior to the hostilities. Some were drafted, and soon we began hearing about those who had been wounded or killed. My cousin announced before he left for the military that he didn't think he'd return. He was right. That experience started me thinking that mind can shape events and that thoughts can become self-fulfilling prophesies. Those who are determined to survive and say so, often do. The opposite frequently is true for those who are convinced they're going to be the victims.

The tragic deaths of young men from towns like Dothan and farming communities like Slocomb brought home the reality of armed conflict. My father, who was getting old, was adamant he didn't want me, his youngest child, running off to war. In any event, I was in no rush to seek action or glory. By my last year in high school, it was clear the war was winding down, and the Allies would be the victors. Rather than take a chance on getting drafted into the army, which I reasoned might mean a long stay in Europe or in the Pacific theater to restore normalcy, the navy looked like a smarter, safer choice.

Our local newspaper, the *Dothan Eagle*, had published a story about how the navy needed radio technicians. Radio technology, which was new and advancing rapidly, interested me. I took the bus to Dothan to ask the navy recruiter, a chief petty officer, how to qualify. He instructed me what to read, a book that was available at the library. If I passed the written test, he told me, I could be inducted as seaman first class, provided the navy still needed radio technicians. The material wasn't particularly difficult. I took the exam and passed.

I graduated from Slocomb High School in 1944, four months shy of my eighteenth birthday. On October 16, 1944, I registered for the draft and was classified 1A. Later on, I reported to Ft. McClellan in Anniston, Alabama, one of the biggest army bases in the country, for physical and other examinations.

At my physical, I was told I didn't pass. I received notification that my health was fine. From the follow-up questions asked at my physical, I deduced that my emotional maturity wasn't deemed sufficient for reasons that weren't explained. I guessed that the military thought I wasn't quite ready to be a soldier and perhaps had decided I could benefit from another few months of "growing up." My induction was delayed for six months. Since I wasn't eager to march off to war, the notice came as good news.

With time on my hands until the military needed me, I applied to work at the Kingan & Company slaughterhouse in Dothan, the town's biggest private employer. Kingan's workforce numbered fifty to sixty people; they slaughtered animals brought to them by local farmers, cut the carcasses into pieces, and then further sliced them into hams, bacon, and cuts of beef, which were then shipped to stores.

My job was to supervise the scales on which the animals stood before they were slaughtered and to record their weight. The number of pounds, multiplied by the prevailing price for beef or pork "on the hoof," determined what Kingan paid the farmer.

The meat products from Kingan's Dothan plant were distributed to grocery stores roughly forty or fifty miles in every direction. That circumference defined the distance beyond which meat would spoil before it could be delivered to consumers since refrigerated trucks and train cars weren't yet common.

Farmers brought livestock to the plant whenever they needed money, rather than at a set time of the year. I was assigned to a crew that received the animals. A young black boy named Willie was responsible for driving them to the scale; another black boy named Jessie took them to be slaughtered. They both called me "Mr. Clyde," according to the custom of how blacks were expected to address whites in those days.

Because I didn't drive and the bus schedule didn't align with my schedule at work, I lived in a rented room near the plant with two other fellows. The cost was $3 a week, plus the cost of eating in cheap restaurants. I took the bus home every weekend.

The workforce at the Kingan plant consisted of whites and blacks. White folks and black folks got along most of the time in rural Alabama, as long as the rigid code of behavior and system of laws that separated the races, commonly known as Jim Crow, was observed. It was commonly understood among whites that blacks occupied a rung of society somewhere below them. Whites and blacks didn't sit together on the bus or study together at the same schools. White mortuaries wouldn't pick up a black body, a fact I witnessed one day when a hearse from the town's white funeral home refused to pick up a black shooting victim from the roadway.

Recalling the laws and customs of race relations during my youth in the South, the world in which I was raised strikes me faraway and remote. At that time it was reality, however, and wouldn't be questioned broadly and publicly until the civil rights movement gained momentum twenty years later.

After a few months working at Kingan, my draft date was fast approaching. The short delay in my induction turned out to be extremely significant, since the navy had let me know that it no longer needed radio technicians. By May 1945, the war was over in Europe and would be over a few months later in the Pacific. Had I been drafted six months earlier, I might have ended up in combat in Europe or in the Pacific.

I and about twenty-five other recruits swore our oaths in Birmingham on August 18, 1945, about two hundred miles north of Slocomb, and shipped out by train to Chicago. The navy operated one of its biggest training bases just north of the city. For some reason, maybe because I was from a farm and presumed to be more responsible than the city boys, the officer put me in charge of my group, an assignment that made me feel important, maybe even gave me a bit of swagger. Did I display at a young age a bit of "leadership gene," a notion that management science would identify years later? I'm not sure.

Prior to my trip North, I'd never been farther from home than Montgomery, about a hundred miles from our farm. Our train stopped in Nashville and Louisville and finally in Chicago. Just north of the city, a few blocks from Lake Michigan, lay the sprawling Great Lakes Naval Station. I felt a surge of excitement and wonder with each new sight; the experience of getting off a train and walking through a big city had been beyond my imagination just a few weeks earlier on the farm.

Within days, the navy assigned me to classes for training as a clerk, teaching me about veteran benefits and how to interview sailors who were being discharged from the service. With the war over, hundreds of thousands of sailors were returning from service, many from battle overseas; they were passing through our base to return equipment and be debriefed prior to being sent home. More than a few had been overseas for several years. Some had been wounded and shell-shocked. I was instructed to explain GI benefits and how to gain access to medical care or to a chaplain, if they needed one.

For a bashful Southerner, meeting and interviewing thousands of returning veterans from across the country and all walks of life was a priceless experience. To answer questions confidently I had to know facts and to convey information concisely and authoritatively. My job was to be knowledgeable and reassuring. I felt exceptionally satisfied and proud to assist sailors who had served their country, to ease their return to civilian life and to arm them with confidence and optimism.

The pride I felt serving my country assuaged the derogatory talk I had heard about Alabamans as a child. We often read in the newspapers or heard on the radio that our state was supposed to be rural and backward, its people poor and ignorant. Since the Civil War, much of the South's economy depended on farming. Perhaps social scientists had compiled metrics or produced studies showing how we lagged behind other states, especially in educational achievement, but we didn't recognize ourselves as the stereotypical bumpkins the outside world made us out to be. As I conversed with more and more sailors from all kinds of backgrounds, I understood that I had no reason to feel inferior or less intelligent than any of them.

My Southern accent often would prompt a question or remark from a fellow sailor or one of the commanding officers about where I was from. The questions never bothered me, because I was proud of my home. But I also found myself listening to how others spoke and, perhaps unconsciously, trying to articulate words as they did. Over the years my southern accent would grow fainter and less prominent until it hardly was recognized as such. Some who heard me speak guessed I was from Missouri or Kentucky, rather than the Deep South.

My job as an interviewer for the navy wasn't only interesting; it came wrapped in a tremendous perk: I was located just on the outskirts of Chicago, one of the great cities of the world. As a clerk, I belonged to what the navy called "ship's company" and was authorized to leave the base whenever my work was complete. My buddies and I took advantage of this privilege prodigiously. Our pay provided us a little money, so we could eat in restaurants and go to the theater. Wearing a uniform in 1945, in the midst of the Allied victory, bestowed celebrity status. Civilians in Chicago were tremendously warm, grateful, and polite to anyone in uniform, offering us meals, drinks, hotel rooms, and tickets. As far as they knew, I could have just returned from Iwo Jima, and they didn't seem to mind a bit when I told them that my battle station was a desk and a typewriter up the road at Great Lakes.

I was barely twenty years old, and many good things had already happened for me. They were early examples of a good fortune that would follow me for my whole life. For reasons I can't explain, I seemed to attract people who were willing to befriend me, to follow my lead in business, and to do favors for me that weren't required.

Anton Anosti, my best buddy in the navy, invited me to his home in Milwaukee on the weekends. His father was an architect. I knew what an architect did but never had met one. An officer at the base, who had been a college professor in civilian life, took me to his home in Chicago to spend time with his wife and family. How would I, a boy who had been weighing hogs in Dothan a few months earlier, otherwise have had a chance to meet a college professor or to roam a city like Chicago?

One day a few months into my service at Great Lakes, my commanding officer, Lt. Com. John R. Hammack, inquired whether I had yet taken an extended leave, or "liberty," as the navy called it. I replied that I wasn't yet eligible.

He immediately ordered his assistant to issue me two consecutive three-day leaves—which, technically, he wasn't supposed to do—so I could travel home and visit my folks.

That leave was a small example of the type of good fortune or blessing, if you will, that would follow me throughout my life. I've never met anyone who benefitted from these random acts of kindness as I did. Without bidding or request on my part, supervisors, mentors, and often even strangers would single me out to receive a favor or advantage. I've struggled to understand why these events have happened to me so often, out of the blue, and without any apparent reason. One of my close friends and colleagues later in life insisted I was blessed with a "magnetism" (as he called it) that drew people and influenced them in my favor. Obviously, I can't be objective about his judgment; I can only guess that's what it means to live a charmed life.

I came home to a warm welcome from my family, albeit to distressing news: my mother reported that my father's health was poor. He had suffered a stroke. Because the war was over, my commanding officer, upon hearing about my father's health, decided I might as well be discharged.

"You have done enough for your country," he said. "Go home and take care of your family." Nine months after leaving Slocomb, I was on my way back. My military career had been short, sweet, and powerfully maturing.

In a very short time I'd undergone a profound transformation. No longer the shy farm boy that lacked self-confidence, I suddenly felt it was the most natural thing in the world to look people in the eye and to speak my mind directly.

By the time I reached our farm near Slocomb, my father was growing stronger by the day. My brother Wilburn had the operations of the farm well in hand, so I was free to choose my next step. I didn't waste any time. Campbell Business College in Dothan or the University of Alabama in Tuscaloosa looked like obvious choices, especially because I knew from explaining a thousand times to other veterans how easily the GI bill would cover the cost of my studies.

Since classes didn't start until the fall, I bought a bus ticket to Orlando, intending to pick citrus for a few months and earn money for school. While waiting at the station in Dothan for the Orlando bus to arrive, I heard a voice. "Clyde, is that you?"

It was Milton Newton. Amazingly, the superintendent of the Kingan plant, where I'd worked briefly before the navy, happened to be standing near the bus station and recognized me from my brief employment there.

"When are you coming back to the plant?" he asked. It turned out to be one of those serendipitous, life-changing moments. I explained my plans to pick fruit in Orlando.

"Oh, that's a big mistake, son," he said. "Come on down to the plant tomorrow morning, and I'll show you why returning to Kingan is the smartest thing you can do."

No doubt Kingan already was feeling the upswing in post-war economic demand that was bringing with it a growing need for labor. Whatever Kingan had to offer, I reasoned, it probably was better than slaving in the hot sun, picking fruit and vegetables. College would still be available to me in the fall.

I turned in my bus ticket for a refund. The next morning I reported to the plant where I was hired as chief clerk at a salary of $30 a week. It felt like a pretty good paycheck. My job was collecting numbers, all sorts of information from a factory's manufacturing operations—"data" in today's jargon. Numbers aren't sexy—a word I never would have used in those days—but they are the heart and soul of what makes a business tick. And it felt good to return to familiar surroundings.

Fellow workers at the plant who remembered me from the previous year welcomed me back, inquired about my adventures in the navy, and commented how much more confident and secure I seemed than the boy who was weighing hogs less than a year earlier. Travel, responsibilities, and friendships with people unlike those from my hometown had been the ingredients to create in me worldliness not all that common in Dothan, Alabama.

One of the managers at Kingan said, "Clyde, I don't know what happened to you in the navy. It's as if you've grown up ten years overnight."

The manager's comment filled me with joy. I didn't understand at that moment his comment also meant that Kingan viewed me in a far different light with regard to my future than as a teenager weighing hogs.

CHAPTER 2

My Career Begins, Pencil in Hand

My job as clerk at the Kingan slaughterhouse, which started shortly after my discharge from the navy, suited me so well that I soon more or less stopped thinking about attending college. Once I was earning a salary, why give that up?

I watched my fellow workers at Kingan as they sawed carcasses into pieces, sliced cuts of meat, hauled tools, herded animals, and loaded trucks. By the end of the day they were exhausted. My tools were a pencil and a notebook. I was getting more and more comfortable roaming the plant, collecting, codifying, and crunching numbers. My bosses needed to know precisely how many hogs were processed each day, how many cattle and how many pounds of meat were shipped. They wanted to identify trends, hours worked, amount of each product purchased, and shipping costs.

My lessons at school and duties in the navy had prepared me well. I created and organized reports for our managers and sent copies to headquarters in Indianapolis. Kingan's other plants around the U.S. employed clerks like me, who did the same. Accurate, up-to-date, and easily accessible information was vital for managing a business and keeping it profitable as it grew to larger and larger scale. Little by little, I was becoming familiar with the key performance indicators critical to running a meat business.

Kingan had begun as a family enterprise in Belfast, Ireland. The company opened a branch in Indianapolis in 1863, becoming a major supplier to the Union army and a destination for Irish immigrants who needed a job. Later on, Kingan expanded throughout the United States, eventually growing into a publicly owned corporation. The company's hams, bacon, and pork products were sold at retailers all over the country under the Kingan's Reliable brand, which was well known by consumers. Kingan family members still populated management.

It was pretty much an open secret that our plant was struggling in comparison to others operated by the company. I was too inexperienced to understand why. One day we were told that a gentleman from Kingan headquarters by the name of Dan Cassidy would be arriving. Whenever someone arrived from headquarters, it was a big deal, an occasion to tidy up the operations and to look sharp. Since the plant wasn't doing well, this visit took on special importance.

Mr. Cassidy, as I addressed him initially, was Kingan's in-house expert on the subject of so-called time-motion studies, a method of analyzing jobs and manufacturing processes to make them safer, easier on the workers, and, most importantly, efficient. As clerk, it was my job to show Mr. Cassidy around the plant and to familiarize him with our people and departments. He had come to Dothan to study ways of improving efficiency, in an effort to make the plant more profitable.

He and I hit it off right away, though I didn't foresee how much impact this association would have on my career. Mr. Cassidy was scheduled to spend several months at the plant. During that time, he took a room at the Houston Hotel in Dothan. The hotel didn't yet own a radio. As such, he was disappointed, because he was an avid football fan and loved listening to college games during his free time on Saturday afternoon. I volunteered to bring him my radio. He responded by inviting me to listen to the game with him.

I still didn't care much about sports. In the course of the visits, he asked questions, and we would discuss trouble spots at the plant, which were more numerous than our managers had realized. As his project to improve operations grew in scope and our working relationship deepened, he asked that I be assigned to assist him.

The methods Mr. Cassidy brought to the plant lay very much in the vanguard of what was trendy in business. The concept of optimizing the efficiency of manufacturing processes, as well as individual factory jobs, stemmed from pioneering research by Frederick Winslow Taylor and by Frank and Lillian Gilbreth. (The Gilbreths were celebrated in the 1950s for their autobiographical book, *Cheaper by the Dozen*.) By measuring and timing tasks and processes, jobs could be revised and rearranged to optimum productivity—not just for the sake of more output, but also to minimize effort and increase safety.

Accurate data, quickly becoming my specialty, was fundamental to precise analysis; hence, Mr. Cassidy's decision to recruit me created a logical fit for our jobs. The experience of assisting him proved invaluable, introducing me to the idea that factory-floor problems, no matter how complex, were much easier to solve once they were divided into pieces. The pieces could be identified and analyzed separately; then it was often quite obvious to see which needed overhaul or replacement.

The step that actually created a problem or bottleneck often seemed rather insignificant at first. The most important insight wasn't the knowledge *how* to fix but rather identifying exactly *what* must be fixed.

As the time-motion program got fully under way, Mr. Cassidy's stint in Dothan was drawing to a close. He announced his intention to hire a fellow named Chauncey Marks to run the program, with me as Marks's assistant. I was terribly proud and gratified that Mr. Cassidy and my bosses at the plant were so confident about me.

Unfortunately, the new head of time-study struggled. A few months after he was hired, Mr. Marks was discharged, leaving me to run the program.

I wish our efforts had borne more fruit. The modifications and changes fell short of elevating the Dothan plant to the standard expected by Kingan executives in Indianapolis. In 1946, the company decided to give up its lease for the plant, which later would be picked up by Wilson, another huge national meatpacking concern.

My future suddenly appeared uncertain. I was just twenty years old, with a high school diploma, a short stretch in the navy, and less than two years on the job. My days in the meat business, it seemed, were over as quickly as they had begun. I started to think about college again.

To my surprise, my boss summoned me to his office. "Hey, Clyde," he said, "the company wants to know if you'd be interested in a transfer to another Kingan plant."

"Yes, sir," I responded instantly. "Anywhere you want to send me." Whatever else I was, I was certainly eager.

After returning from the navy and finding a job, I had wrongly assumed the rest of my life would be mapped out in Dothan. Events suddenly were unfolding in a way I would have thought unlikely, if not impossible: I was about to leave my home and the South again, this time for good.

CHAPTER 3

Northward to Indiana

My hospitality toward Dan Cassidy and enthusiasm assisting him with the time-motion studies at the plant undoubtedly played a role in my transfer North in the wake of Kingan's shutdown in Dothan. Kingan could have terminated me, an inexperienced clerk, without a second thought. I was hardly essential: what I didn't know about business and life, not to mention the meat business, could fill an encyclopedia.

But I did have something going for me, my can-do attitude. I wasn't trying to be noticed, but it evidently had caught Mr. Cassidy's attention and duly been noted and reported to headquarters in Indianapolis. He believed I could be an asset to the company and would fit in well at one of its plants.

Despite having no college education, my literacy from a strong high school background, aptitude with numbers, and ability to produce clear, easily understood reports singled me out as potentially useful in the eyes of Kingan managers. My best subjects at Slocomb High School had been math and science. Ida Bell Phinney, a favorite teacher, possessed a special talent for explaining our lessons so they could be understood. With the nation at war, she had realized the practical benefits that schooling would have for a soldier. She offered tutorials in the evenings, mainly attended by the boys, so that those who were drafted or volunteered would be well prepared for military service, at least intellectually, whether they were clerks like me, pilots, or tank commanders. Her classes had paid off for me in the navy and, again, in my first job.

I worried that saying good-bye to my parents for an indefinite period of time would be emotional, and I was right. I had been living in a rented room while working in Dothan, traveling home to our farm every weekend by bus. My mother made a big fuss about my transfer, taking pains to remark that she was getting old and I would be departing, who knows when to return.

My father told her to "leave the boy alone." He understood that I had to live my own life and find my destiny. Leaving home didn't in any way diminish the importance of my family. They were dear to me and always would remain so.

The city was still dark the morning of departure from Dothan, when I walked from 218 South Foster Street to the railroad station, carrying one small bag of belongings.

As I waited for the train north, eager for the fresh, new experiences that awaited me, I thought about how my upbringing and schooling, capped by my experience in the navy and the good fortune to be employed, all had created a pathway to a world I hardly knew existed and was now beckoning me. The train from Miami to Chicago, pulled by two enormous steam locomotives, stopped for passengers in Dothan at 4:00 a.m. About twelve hours later it arrived in Indianapolis, where I disembarked.

Indianapolis, an immense, bustling city compared to Dothan, might have overwhelmed me if I hadn't already experienced Chicago two years earlier while in the navy. This was the place on Indiana's White River where the Kingan family of Belfast decided to open a branch of its meatpacking enterprise. Giddy with confidence and anticipation for whatever lay ahead at Kingan headquarters, I found a hotel and checked in at the princely rate of $3 a night.

The next morning I awoke early, dressed in a freshly-pressed suit, white shirt, and tie and walked along the White River for an hour. I strode into Kingan's lobby at the stroke of 8:00 a.m. and, as instructed, asked to see George Munce, the vice president of operations.

A heavyset man who had been the superintendent of operations in Richmond, Munce was kind and asked me if I had received a cash advance before leaving Dothan. When I told him no, he sent his secretary for some money immediately. I was so green it never occurred to me that I had to account for the money and reimburse the company. Two years later a secretary to Kingan's president found the discrepancy and helped me to resolve it.

Kingan had considered two locations for its newest transferee, a meatpacking plant in Philadelphia and one in Storm Lake, Iowa. Based on Dan Cassidy's recommendation, Munce explained, the company had decided on Storm Lake, the newest and most modern the company had built since the war. He scheduled me to meet a few of the company's executives. The vice presidents, having heard reports about me, wanted to see the new boy for themselves and invited me to dinner.

One of the most important of these executives was Thomas Sinclair, general manager of the Kingan plant in Indianapolis. The Sinclairs also had owned a meatpacking business in Ireland, which had merged with Kingan. An experienced executive in his early forties, he belonged to the firm's founding family. His vast knowledge and excellent judgment were well suited to the complexities and ever-changing nature of the meat business. Our paths would cross again. Within a few days, in May of 1947, he sent me on my way west to Iowa and the Storm Lake plant.

Storm Lake, plunked roughly between Des Moines and Sioux City in the middle of Iowa farm country, was much more like rural Alabama and familiar to me than Indianapolis. My job title, though I'd never taken a college class, was time-study engineer. I reported to Ralph Bradley, head of that department.

Getting the lay of the land in such a small rural town wasn't difficult. The fact I didn't have much money dictated that my life would be simple: Kingan paid me $55 a week. My rented room cost $10 a week, which left me very little for expenses and pocket money. Knowing no one and with no obligations other than to perform well at the plant, I wore out the public library and the movie theater.

Truth be told, Kingan wasn't paying me enough to live. Rather than complain, I wrote to Mr. Cassidy to report that I was doing fine since my savings allowed me to pay my bills. Once the savings were gone, I explained, I would be returning to Dothan. My salary was raised immediately.

A coworker at the plant, recognizing that I was alone and knew no one, kindly introduced me to an elderly widow in town, Honey Miller, who had a room to let. The late George Miller, her husband, had owned the hardware store in town and had done well with it. Searching for a hobby in retirement, George had fulfilled his lifelong dream of earning a pilot's license and, tragically, was killed in an accident, at the controls of a plane.

Without a husband and childless, Honey rented me a room and befriended me. I suppose I offered some company, as well as extra income. She often invited me to eat with her, teaching me a great deal about manners and social etiquette. As a Southern farm boy I was extremely polite and respectful, but I'd never learned the niceties of how to order food at a restaurant, how to make small talk at a party, or the proper mode of dress for different business and social occasions. Honey taught me a million things I didn't know and had to learn, in order to blend with the polished managers and executives I was increasingly meeting in the course of my job. We became friends.

After dinner we often sat in her living room listening to the radio. That's where we were in the summer of 1948, during Thomas Dewey's acceptance speech for the Republican nomination during his second unsuccessful run for the presidency. "I come to you unfettered!" Dewey thundered during the broadcast, a remarkably silly phrase for a presidential candidate, if I'd ever heard one.

****

For all its apparent isolation, the Storm Lake plant took on a strategic importance for Kingan due to its location, about 1,300 miles from the East Coast and about 1,700 miles from the West Coast of the United States. Surrounding Buena Vista County was one of the top hog-producing centers in the country, affording the company a convenient location from which to buy animals and to distribute pork products to a large number of consumers.

The plant manager at Storm Lake was Tom Nash, a wealthy man who once had owned his own meatpacking plant. I had been sent by Kingan management in Indianapolis to search for ways to make his plant more efficient. My salary represented overhead against the plant's revenue and counted against its profit—a metric on which he was judged. Soon after arriving, Nash ordered me to reorganize the plant parking lot and draw new lines to designate spaces for the workers, which I considered a "make work" assignment, of little or no importance. I had many more important priorities, but if that's what he ordered, I wasn't about to argue.

"Sure," I told him. "How about if I come in on Sunday and get the parking lot done for you?"

Nash understood what I was implying, and he dropped the parking lot idea. My diplomacy had won the day. He and I got along famously.

One year in Storm Lake flew by quickly. I enjoyed and was settling into my new responsibilities, home, and friends. George Munce, on a visit to the plant, called me one day into an office to deliver shocking news: Dan Cassidy had suffered a stroke.

"We're not sure about his recovery," said Munce, "but we know he'll definitely be out for a minimum of several months. We want you to come to Indianapolis and run his office until he returns."

I was saddened to hear that my mentor and friend had been stricken.

The next day I caught the train to Indianapolis, not knowing when or if I would return.

Three weeks later, Dan—by this time we were on a first-name basis—succumbed to his illness. It was a blow to his family, to me, and to Kingan.

I was touched and honored when Dan's widow, Sarah, asked me to be a pallbearer at his funeral. A few days after the funeral, she called me to come out to the house. Dan had an extensive library, which she asked me to take. I wish I could have accepted. I was living at the YMCA and had no place to put the books.

As so often the case in life, the closing of one door represented the opening of another. In light of Dan's death, the company asked me to leave Storm Lake and accept the post of time-study engineer, with responsibility for time-studies of all pork operations at Kingan's Indianapolis plant. Indy was one of the largest meatpacking plants in the country, with over a thousand workers. I was exhilarated by the size and scope of this new assignment.

The company obviously was pleased with my progress. After a year of seasoning in Storm Lake, I was back under the wing of Mr. Sinclair, my second key mentor after Dan and one of the most important executives at the company. At home on the farm my relatives would have described me as having landed in "high cotton."

The meat business, Sinclair explained to me, was responding rapidly to shifting consumer tastes and economic forces. Kingan was struggling to keep up. Prior to the war, a shopper usually ordered lunch meat from a grocer or butcher according to a specific weight; the clerk then sliced and prepared the order from a very large piece of meat and wrapped it. This took time and effort, which added to the grocer's cost. In the meantime, meatpackers increasingly were producing packages of pre-sliced meat. Consumers more and more were perfectly content to buy packaged lunchmeat at supermarkets, which were growing larger and rapidly replacing small neighborhood groceries.

Kingan had been packaging sliced luncheon meat but was losing out to lower-priced competition. Sinclair ordered me to determine our company's costs for producing specific lunchmeat products and to figure out how we might meet or beat the competition.

"Go find out how much it costs us to slice deli loaves," he commanded. "The competition is beating our price on the street every time."

Figuring out costs of product, production, and packaging would make us competitive and increase sales in order to gain a bigger share of the market. Using the skills I'd learned working for Dan, I figured out that our costs were ten cents per pound higher than other manufacturers, a considerable disparity.

When I reported to Sinclair that we had to find a way to cut the cost in order to compete, his response was crisp. "Make it happen." I did. The assignments kept coming.

I was learning a lot about the meat business spending time with "Mr. Sinclair," as I called him, and what it meant to be an executive. He took me with him to the barbershop and to the stockyards, talking all the while about buying animals, processing them and distributing meat.

Learning the ins and outs of Kingan's Indianapolis factory occupied most of my time for the first few months. The concepts were straightforward and fairly easy to understand, but I had to absorb a new language filled with words whose meanings were unclear. When engineers unfurled blueprints I was more or less lost. The finance people threw around terms like "equity" and "amortization." My lack of college-level knowledge was beginning to interfere with growing responsibilities that required me to understand and discuss technical and financial concepts.

The solution was obvious: more education. Fortunately, central Indiana was full of great colleges offering classes for part-time students, many of whom—like me—were working in the day and studying in the evenings. Earning an academic degree or credential wasn't my goal. I needed knowledge, pure and simple. First on my educational agenda was a course at Lain Drafting College that taught me how to read a blueprint. I took a basic engineering course at Purdue and several accounting courses at Butler.

In short order, I was able to connect the dots among principles of manufacturing, accounting, engineering, and finance as they related to the meatpacking business. The experience I had gained in a few years on the job was reinforced by academic knowledge. As I became comfortable with the language of the plant, I was learning to "howl with the pack."

Kingan executives noticed and approved. They soon appointed me chief clerk for the Indianapolis plant, supervising twenty clerks who reported to me.

As chief clerk, I occasionally double-checked inventory numbers for accuracy, especially if they looked wrong. On one occasion, a union steward lodged a complaint—a "grievance," in union-speak—against me for performing duties that technically were assigned to the clerks. It was an example of the control over the plants that unions exerted. Nothing came of the grievance, because the clerks weren't interested in making an issue of it. But the episode showed how managements in the meatpacking business often struggled against the union over petty issues of power and control.

Kingan's decision a few years earlier to pull out of Dothan, followed by the urgent cost-cutting ordered by Sinclair, had provided me ample hints as to the company's longstanding and growing competitive difficulties in the meatpacking business. The post-war period in the United States was one of rapid growth and innovation. Americans were becoming more numerous, as well as more prosperous. As a result, they could afford to eat better and added more meat to their diets.

Meatpacking in the first part of the century had been an inviting business for those with little capital. The barriers to entry were low. An entrepreneur only needed access to livestock, sharp cutting tools, a workforce, and a slaughterhouse. Since the labor unions in cities like Indianapolis had been successful in organizing campaigns, operators increasingly were seeking locations away from union strongholds where they could pay the prevailing wage.

My job at the Indianapolis plant, on top of my studies, occupied all of my time. Without family nearby, I had arrived at my mid-twenties with no companion, no one to share my life. Truth be told, I was about as inexperienced as a man could be when it came to matters of the heart: growing up in Slocomb I'd kept pretty much to myself. I'd never had a girlfriend in high school and not so much as a date before the age of twenty-one.

One day in 1951 at the Mills Hotel, the residence hotel in Indianapolis where I was renting a room, I struck up a casual conversation with a woman in the lobby. She asked me if I was dating anyone. When I told her I wasn't, she described a "beautiful girl" who lived nearby with her mother and didn't have a boyfriend. Automatically, because it seemed like the polite thing to do, I extended an invitation to the three of them to come by one afternoon for a visit.

Patricia Joann Thomas was a registered nurse, employed by the "communicable diseases" ward at the local hospital. She mostly cared for victims of polio, infantile paralysis, a virus-borne disease that was terrifying the nation. Polio wouldn't be controlled until 1955 when Dr. Jonas Salk announced the invention of a vaccine. In the meantime, the medical world had its hands full with the victims.

Patricia's parents had been divorced when she was young. But she and I shared a few things in common. She grew up on a farm in southern Indiana, a region that was more similar in culture to the South than to the

Midwest. Three years my junior, we discovered that we had studied from the same textbooks in school.

The first time we met on the big porch that encircled my hotel, she was wearing a striking red sweater that delightfully set off her charming figure. One of the key elements for any relationship is attraction, and I was attracted.

We were both quite busy during the week, she at the hospital and I with work and night classes. I suggested we take the train to South Bend the following Saturday to watch a Notre Dame football game. Our first date consisting of two train rides and a college football game lasted about twelve hours. Twelve hours is a long first date if you're not enjoying yourself. I knew from that day we were right for each other.

For the next year our dates were mostly long Sunday drives across the Indiana countryside. She packed a picnic lunch, and we'd climb into my car, a used 1951 Plymouth, that I'd bought for $1,695. I'd bought that car without a license or insurance and drove it home from the dealership without ever having driven on a public road.

It was obvious to both of us we were a great match and meant for one another. We were married on October 30, 1952. Clarence and Catherine Mills, owners of the Mills Hotel, stood in for my parents. After the ceremony at the house I'd rented for us, they drove us to Cincinnati for dinner and a show.

We settled down the same night, following the show, to a blissful married life in our home at 4128 East Twelfth Street, on the outskirts of Indianapolis. Pat was a delightful companion and a dedicated homemaker. Our son David was born in 1953; our daughter Margaret followed in 1957. Pat proved to be an excellent mother as well, taking primary and diligent responsibility for rearing the children. One night, I returned from the plant after midnight to find Pat and our pediatrician caring for David, who was quite ill with some childhood ailment that I don't recall. Her nurse's training and connections to the medical community had proved invaluable.

The business pressures at the Kingan factory didn't afford me as much time as I wanted to spend with my wife and children. Rival meatpackers were steadily becoming more formidable. Those that could figure out how to shave pennies of cost here and there were reinvesting savings into new technology such as diesel-powered refrigeration in railcars, which were replacing the ice-filled railcars invented in the nineteenth century. The more nimble marketers fought (and sometimes bribed) their way onto retailer's shelves and into their meat departments.

One of Kingan's toughest adversaries was Detroit-based Hygrade

Food Products. Because of Hygrade's close proximity to Indianapolis, the two companies constantly battled for the same customers. A showdown appeared likely. It happened in 1952 when smaller Hygrade ($137 million in sales) acquired the larger Kingan ($214 million in sales).

Samuel Slotkin had founded Hygrade in 1914 in New York. A colorful figure once profiled by *The New Yorker* magazine, Slotkin gave up his youthful ambition to be a painter in favor of the meat business. He converted the company into a public corporation in 1926 and was able to buy many bankrupt meat businesses in the Depression. Slotkin explained, a touch facetiously, that he regarded his company to be a work of art more than an enterprise.

As he told *Time* magazine, in a second profile, "I am not grubbing for money. I am painting a picture as a life work. Every day I put in a brush stroke or two."

The deal to buy Kingan created the nation's fifth-largest meatpacking company. The Kingan name would soon disappear. Hygrade was making its mark as an up-and-coming, expanding food-processing empire—and my new employer.

CHAPTER 4

Moving Up the Ladder in Indianapolis

Hygrade and Kingan were mirror images of one another, except in one key respect. Both operated slaughterhouses and manufacturing plants over large portions of the country. Both cranked out meat products, as well as cheese. The main difference was that Hygrade made money and Kingan didn't.

Hugo Slotkin, the son of Hygrade's founder and its president, sent Harry Staub, one of the company's top executives, to Indianapolis from Detroit to run Kingan's operations until they were integrated into Hygrade's. Staub brought along an assistant secretary of the corporation, Joe Connors, to make sense of Kingan's numbers. After examining Kingan's books, Staub concluded the information he was getting was confusing and inconsistent, which created a barrier to understanding snafus and inefficiencies and how to fix them. Kingan's inability to get a clear picture of its own operations probably lay at the heart of why it hadn't been sufficiently profitable and, ultimately, why it became the prey of another meatpacking company.

Although I was the chief clerk, Connors initially was relying on several sources for information. He soon discovered, however, that the numbers I provided were consistently reliable, allowing him to decipher the riddle of Kingan's suboptimal performance. In short order, I was tapped as Connors's "go-to" guy for quick, accurate reporting about how the plant's processes were performing.

My reports uncovered a disturbing trend. We were conducting countless time-motion studies filled with insights into potential productivity improvements, but little seemed to change. We couldn't understand why improvement was elusive. Were foremen and managers ignoring us? We held discussions and probed deeper.

Finally, it became obvious that managers weren't obstinate; they simply didn't understand the numbers we were furnishing. Worse, they didn't know how to use them as a guide for improving productivity. Connors concurred with my recommendation that I meet weekly with managers during the lunch break to dissect and explain the results of our studies and to instruct them, step by step, what to do.

The weekly skull sessions evolved into a ritual. Over the next five years the time-motion sessions, plus the lunchtime meetings for explanation of their significance and suggested improvements, delivered steadily higher productivity for Hygrade at the Indianapolis plant. By 1957, the place was performing well.

One day in May 1957, as we were about to start our weekly meeting, a visitor peeked into the room. I recognized him from his photographs in meat industry trade publications. It was Hugo Slotkin, on an inspection tour from Detroit.

"Mr. Slotkin, would you like to join our meeting?" I asked, beckoning him toward me.

"No, no," he replied, signaling me with his hands to proceed. The motion with his hands was a characteristic gesture, one I would come to know very well over the years. He stood silently at the back of the room, watching while I reviewed the week's numbers with the managers. As usual, we discussed opportunities to reduce waste and increase output. Years later, Toyota's famous production system received a boatload of publicity for undertaking exactly what we were doing in Indianapolis, constantly tweaking processes and stamping out waste.

When the meeting ended, Slotkin slipped out of the room without saying a word.

What Hygrade's president saw and heard that day must have impressed him, because the next morning I was summoned to Sinclair's office. While others from Kingan management and his family had left after the sale to Hygrade, Sinclair had stayed to run the plant as general manager.

"Clyde, I just got a call from headquarters," he said. "They want you to come to Detroit right away for a management training program."

My astonishment quickly turned into excitement. I'd been quite satisfied and content with my role in Indianapolis, never dreaming that I would be noticed or singled out by top management. Nevertheless, if Hygrade wanted me for management training, I was ready. Within a few weeks, I was commuting to Detroit.

Inviting me for management training was a clear signal that the company had a role in mind for me beyond the level of chief clerk. My upbringing on a small farm taught me to keep my head down, to do your best, and not to be presumptuous. Great opportunities didn't always present themselves, but you had to be ready if they did.

"Hugo Slotkin keeps a black book," Ernest Erickson, Hygrade's vice president of finance, told me. "In it, are the names of people he believes are potential managers. After attending your meeting in Indianapolis, he put your name in the book."

My three-month training course started on the floor of Hygrade's plant on Michigan Avenue in Detroit. Senior managers devised the study regimen, introducing me and others being considered for general management positions to the specifics of the company's culture and its approach to the meat business. Charles E. Bellamy, general manager of Michigan operations was responsible for my training. (Bellamy was a favorite of Hugo Slotkin's; the Hygrade president regularly referred to him as "Charles 'E for Excellence' Bellamy.") Gus Hauff, the chief sausage maker, took me under his wing as well. In the evening, Bellamy, Hauff, and I repaired to a tavern to order a meal, have a few drinks, and review the day's lessons.

After several weeks I traveled to another Hygrade plant, then on to others. The managers taught me the particulars of how the company operated, not just their specific plans. They wanted me to be familiar with the sales staff's duties and how the company marketed its products.

Following several weeks of training, I received a message: Hugo Slotkin wanted to see me Saturday morning on his farm, a magnificent spread near Holly, Michigan.

"My people tell me you're doing fine," he said. "I want you to return to Indianapolis and use what you've learned. You're now in charge of the fresh sausage and lunchmeat operations. This is a big piece of business, it's a mess and must be straightened out."

If Hygrade was to turn its acquisition into a success and justify its investment, it had to turn Kingan's chronically money-losing operations profitable. Kingan's inability to compete with other meatpackers ultimately was the reason its owners had to sell. Hygrade didn't wish to find itself at the mercy of anyone or any other company.

The Indianapolis plant was a sprawling complex with eight divisions: pork, beef, canned meats, canned hams, smoked meats and sliced bacon, dry sausage, fresh sausage and sliced luncheon meats, and inedible operations, each run by a general manager responsible for the profit of the division.

As the newest and youngest general manager, it was the first time I was responsible for financial performance. Nevertheless, I returned to what I had learned about time-motion studies, applying the same principles of dissection and analysis to the sausage and lunchmeat division. The fresh sausage division was the largest and most troubled. My job was to turn it around. I studied each and every process to figure out how to cut cost and improve efficiency. Inevitably, we uncovered steps or redundancies that could be minimized or eliminated, improving the division's output and profitability.

As I pored over the weekly and monthly reports, it was obvious that the division's numbers still weren't nearly what they could be. I considered the operations from every angle and recalled what I'd seen and learned during my three months in Detroit. We could fine-tune processes further to squeeze out more cost and raise manufacturing efficiency. But the most intriguing possibility to improve the bottom line was in sales. By selling more, the division's overall profit margin would rise dramatically.

Everything I'd experienced previously in the meatpacking industry suggested to me that sales mostly were dictated by production, not the other way around. Raw materials arrived "on the hoof." The plant slaughtered cattle and hogs and sold every bit of the animal in one form or another. The number and type of animals slaughtered determined the mix of products sold by the plant. That always had been the logic and mentality of the industry, according to my observation, starting with my first job weighing hogs in Dothan.

In other words, production "pushed" sales. The job of the sales force, which usually was supervised by the plant manager, was to find buyers for what the plant produced.

Profound changes were sweeping the industry and not just in sales. Starting in the last century, livestock used to arrive at big cities like Chicago, New York, Omaha, and Fort Worth and was slaughtered at immense stockyards near population centers or, in some instances, at their center. As transportation and refrigeration improved, the slaughterhouses moved closer to where the animals were raised and shipped carcasses and half-carcasses to butchers. The butchers created cuts of meat from sides and sold them to consumers.

The next big evolution was processing and packaging, which allowed products like hot dogs, bacon, and sliced luncheon meat to be shipped in boxes long distances, directly to retailers.

I could see how the industry was developing quickly in new and different directions and that the operations Hygrade bought from Kingan weren't keeping up with the latest trends. Sales should have been "pulling" output from the plant. For example, if stores and customers were demanding bologna and paying a premium price for it, the plant might yield more profit by adjusting operations so as to optimize bologna production.

A few months following my return from Detroit, Hugo Slotkin arrived again in Indianapolis for one of his periodic reviews. After a meeting with managers, Hygrade's president pulled me aside to ask how my new assignment was progressing.

"We've improved profits," I said. "But to get the kind of results I know the company expects, we have to improve sales. We're just not selling enough."

Slotkin thought about what I'd said for a moment and replied, "Then go out and get more sales."

I had had no experience in sales. Just like that, Slotkin authorized me responsible for several Hygrade salesmen calling on retailers across the Midwest.

As I considered what the salesmen were doing and how to increase their output, my instinct once more was to rely on my time-motion training, to divide the salesmen's activities into components and to analyze their duties from the standpoint of cost and performance. One way to think about their sales would have been to scrutinize results from the previous year, then find a way to improve that baseline. But I don't believe much in the status quo; besides, there was no reason to assume the previous year's numbers were remotely valid in terms of what the division should be selling.

I decided first to look at the cost of keeping each salesman on the payroll. Logic told me that that each salesman's output, in terms of revenue from sausage and lunchmeat, should at least cover his cost to the company, in terms of salary and benefits. I collected the numbers and assigned each salesman a goal based on that analysis, explaining that if they couldn't meet them, the accounts would be realigned and sales positions eliminated. They got the message, and everyone's output increased rapidly. I only had to eliminate one sales position for insufficient output, but the division's sales performance improved significantly. Profits rose noticeably.

Running the sausage division in Indianapolis for four years proved invaluable on-the-job training, sharpening my managerial skills and teaching me what I needed to know about running a big meatpacking plant. Not only had I rearranged the way the salesmen operated, I took it upon myself to visit customers, accompany salesmen on their calls, and drop into stores anonymously on Saturdays and after work to discover more about shoppers, as well as how our products were displayed. I was hungry for every insight or bit of information that might bear on the division's performance.

In 1961, Bellamy, who by then was vice president of Hygrade's Michigan operations, called to offer me the chance to manage an entire plant myself, the company's Heidelberg operations in Detroit. It was named for the run-down neighborhood where it was located. The building was just off Gratiot, a section of the city once inhabited by German immigrants and after the war by African Americans. Hygrade's Heidelberg plant was known as a specialty plant, manufacturing mainly all-beef frankfurters, Vienna sausage, salami, and corned beef brisket. Unlike other plants, which were becoming more and more automated, this one was from the old school, requiring lots of hand labor. The sausages had to be stuffed into casings manually.

Detroit in the early 1960s was a magnificent city: wealthy, sophisticated, and bustling with enterprise. The automobile industry provided rivers of money for its investors, executives, factory workers, and everyone who plied their trade in the vicinity. General Motors sat atop the heap, the most powerful and impressive corporation on earth. Who could have imagined, in their wildest nightmare, how awfully the city and the industry would collapse within a few short decades?

When I arrived, the Heidelberg operations were running efficiently, which meant managing wasn't particularly difficult. One sore spot was the very low level of cleanliness. I asked the plant engineer to undertake a project to improve sanitation, to which he replied curtly that there was no money in the budget for it. Rather than let the matter drop, I hired one of the men from the neighborhood, put him in charge of cleanup and paid him enough so he could hire whatever helpers he needed to get the job done. I also authorized the purchase of equipment.

The higher-ups at headquarters noticed my initiative and approved. I had never possessed this much responsibility. For the first few weeks on the job, it thrilled me to be in charge and to make decisions. But the feeling didn't last long. A year went by; fewer and fewer problems needed to be solved, and profitability was fine. My predecessor obviously had left the place in decent shape. I felt like a caretaker. Unlike the job in Indianapolis, I had no role in sales.

Truth be told, I was bored. But I found ways to keep myself busy.

The promotion to plant manager from department head initially had felt like a feather in my cap. But the new job didn't necessarily mean that there would be more advancement. All of us recognized that Hygrade remained a company dominated by the Slotkin family. Hugo Slotkin's sons and nephews occupied many key posts, leaving a limited number for outsiders. Further promotions or movement for a nonfamily member seemed unlikely. After an uneventful year or so had dragged by, I decided in the fall of 1963 to let Bellamy know, as diplomatically as possible, that my promotion had proved to be unfulfilling. Running the sausage department in Indianapolis, a step lower on the ladder, had been much more stimulating. From my perspective, I wasn't performing to my potential in a boring job.

At age thirty-six, having spent half my life earning a living, this marked the first time I'd ever grumbled to a superior. The conversation felt awkward. Clearing my throat, I told him, "Mr. Bellamy, I don't belong here." It was the best way I knew to express my thoughts without whining.

Thankfully, Bellamy didn't chew me out or fire me on the spot.

"Let me think about it, and I'll get back to you," he said.

He didn't think long. The next day, his secretary called to say her boss wished to see me that Friday morning at 10:00 a.m. I had no clue what was coming. But my gut told me I had been right to speak up, that an unsatisfying job assignment wasn't good for me or for Hygrade.

As soon as I arrived at headquarters for the meeting I could sense that something was up. Bellamy had sent one of the salesmen to escort me to his office. He greeted me.

"Hello, Clyde, come on in," he said, gesturing for me to sit. "I must apologize, but I don't have much time. We're headed north for the weekend, so this has to be short." Many Detroit-based executives kept houses across northern Michigan, in towns like Petoskey and Charlevoix along the shores of Lake Michigan, where often they retreated with their families for the weekend.

I suppose he could have dressed me down for my impatience and lack of gratitude or delivered a sermon about the unavoidable tedium of some jobs. He might have rebuked me for the audacity to assume Hygrade was in business to provide me an exciting career. He could have reminded me about the paycheck I received regularly and suggested that I best concentrate on performing the tasks assigned to me.

Instead, he handed me a slip of paper. Thank heavens it wasn't pink.

"Effective with this memo you're now the sales manager for Michigan," he said. I was touched and more than a bit thrilled.

Bellamy's patience and trust meant the world to me. As far as I was concerned he had been my teacher and protector, one of the most important persons in my life. Sales manager for Michigan was a big step up for me and for my family.

Though we had only been in Michigan for a year, Pat and I in 1962 had bought a small house in Redford, bordering the city, for $10,000, small by anyone's standards but certainly large enough for the four of us. The red brick house at 8848 Sarasota turned out to be the perfect choice. The schools in Redford were fine; Pat found friends and joined a bowling league, which turned into her passion.

When I first mentioned the house to Bellamy, he replied, smiling, "You're the first person who's ever worked for me that didn't check with me about his future before committing to buy a house."

I guess he liked my self-assurance. Fortunately, Bellamy and other executives noticed that I'd performed well and with enthusiasm after they'd given me sales responsibility in Indianapolis. They must have concluded that I had potential and didn't want to smother my enthusiasm. The new position made me responsible for numerous smaller accounts, the larger supermarket chains remaining under the supervision of higher-ranking executives. Bellamy warned me I was being watched closely and would have to prove myself.

Immediately, I began poring over the sales statistics. The very next week I called a sales meeting and announced to our staff, which probably numbered more than a dozen and less than twenty, that I had high expectations. I've never forgotten that meeting. It was held on November 22, 1963, the day of President John F. Kennedy's assassination. No American alive on that day will forget the profound shock of that event. Notwithstanding the tragedy, all of us had to regroup. I had to learn my new responsibilities quickly and show that I could get results.

Having figured out what we were paying the sales staff, it was obvious that each salesperson would have to be selling at least twenty thousand pounds of meat a week to justify the cost of the department. Unless every salesperson could hit that target, I would have to reduce the number of positions. Taking a page from my playbook in Indianapolis, I began to accompany the salesmen on calls, to see how they operated and to meet the customers.

On one of these occasions I met Sam Feig, vice president and director of the meat department for the Chatham supermarket chain. Feig, an immigrant from Czechoslovakia, had spent time in captivity under the Nazis. He had come to the country with very little and worked his way up in the retail meat business. Although we came from differing backgrounds, we were similar in that we started in our careers with very little.

Sam and I hit it off immediately. He began teaching me everything he knew about supermarket retailing and how various cuts of meat were sold, packaged, priced, and presented to shoppers. The knowledge was precious in helping me to understand how Hygrade's products could be successful and what would cause them to fail.

My new role supervising Hygrade's sales in Michigan, its most important market, stretched my ability, energy, and imagination. How could I have known that my role at the company would grow even larger in scope, complexity, and responsibility? To this day, I'm not sure if I could have advanced beyond sales manager without the hundreds of pearls of wisdom that fell from Sam Feig's lips.

CHAPTER 5

The Original Convenience Food's
Long and Glorious History

The story of an Alabama farm boy's ascent through the ranks of the U.S. meatpacking industry wouldn't be complete without a deeper, richer understanding of that noble nourishment—the hot dog.

The authoritative account of the hot dog's earliest origins has been lost to history. A food sounding very much like the hot dog is described in Homer's *Odyssey*. Centuries later similar fare showed up in central Europe. The practice of cooking pieces of meat encased in an intestine, usually from a sheep, became an item known as frankfurters developed in the German city of the same name five hundred years ago. Another name for the food was wieners, derived from the German name for Austria.

Hot dogs really got rolling, so to speak, in the U.S. in the late nineteenth century, a consequence of tourists trying and liking them when they were served at Chicago's Columbian Exposition in 1893. A few years later, they were first served at baseball games in what became, along with peanuts, beer, and the singing of the national anthem, an enduring and characteristic feature of the great American pastime.

Hot dogs initially were encased in a skin. Later on, they were manufactured as "skinless," which saved on cost. Traditionalists missed the snap of the skin when taking a bite, so specialty manufacturers continued to offer sausages and wieners with natural or artificial skin, usually at a higher price.

The bun turned out to be a nifty innovation as a holder, replacing an earlier practice of simply holding it with an eating utensil or in one's gloved or ungloved hand. I thought of hot dogs as the original convenience food, as much loved for their ease of preparation as for their taste.

In my early days as an employee at the Kingan plant in Dothan, I had learned about all sorts of meat products, including hot dogs, while watching them being made at the plant. Workers using sharp tools cut and hacked at carcasses, wearing metal mesh gloves to protect themselves and to keep from being cut by someone else.

The carcasses mostly yielded the best known and most valuable cuts: steaks, chops, roasts, ribs, and so forth. Workers also shipped large parts of the animal whole or halved, to be further divided at local butcher shops and grocery stores. The Kingan slaughterhouse in Dothan manufactured hot dogs, along with hams, bacon, and many other cuts. The trimmings, pieces left over after dividing a carcass into cuts of meat, were saved for manufacturing hot dogs. We also received trimmings from other plants so that we could make hot dogs, baloney, and processed meats for which we lacked ingredients.

The Kingan plant was a beehive of activity and a place where jobs were much in demand, despite the occasional accident and the gruesomeness of so many dead animals. Jobs that paid cash were scarce during the Great Depression and the war years. To be hired by the slaughterhouse was a plum. Lots of men and women were waiting to fill any openings.

Hot dogs were manufactured from a variety of trimmings—the scraps—which were generated as workers hacked or sawed chilled carcasses into smaller, more easily handled pieces. Some trimmings were pieces of lean muscle; others, like pieces from the belly, contained a high proportion of fat. The proportion of one kind of scrap to another, plus the spices, constituted a formula. The formula was critical to taste, consistency, texture, and "binding quality," its ability to retain a distinctive shape when cooked. Salami had a recipe distinct from that of baloney, knockwurst, and other manufactured products.

Workers ran the trimmings through grinders, bigger versions of the crank-operated tools our mothers and grandmothers used in their kitchens prior to the Cuisinart. The output of the process was an emulsion, not solid and not quite liquid.

After chilling the mixture, workers poured the meaty mix into "stuffers," machines that pushed the substance into long cellulose tubes. A linking machine applied string dividers to the tubes of meat according to the sausage or hot dog's desired length. The long lengths of links arrived at the smokehouse for cooking. Afterward, the casings and strings were stripped: the hot dogs were ready for packaging and shipment.

Kingan's Dothan plant and others that made hot dogs and other products that required a recipe, typically employed a "Wurstmacher," or sausage maker. This top foreman was a key member of plant management, responsible for ensuring that the mix was accurate so that hot dogs and other products were consistent and tasty. The Wurstmacher often was a craftsman of German heritage who had learned the tricks of the trade from his father or some other Wurstmacher, possessing recipes that likely originated in central Europe hundreds of years earlier.

During the Depression, meat of any kind was a luxury. As the country grew more prosperous after World War II, housewives found hot dogs to be a simple, quick, and cost-efficient way to feed their families. Once sold in bulk to the butcher or the supermarket's meat department, they more and more became a packaged item, ready to be grabbed from a chilled display case. As I learned more and gained experience in the meatpacking business, I became more familiar with their central role in an average family's diet. Accordingly, they became more and more important to the food-retailing industry and key to overall profitability for meatpackers.

People moving from the cities to the suburbs found hot dogs desirable as a food that could be prepared quickly and cheaply to feed the family. When the weather turned warm, dinner could be turned into entertainment with the advent of outdoor, portable charcoal grilles.

In the 1950s, hot dogs were becoming more popular as a commercial fast food, warmed on an electric grill and sold at soda fountains, sporting events, and at movie theatres. They were the go-to dish at institutional barbeques and church picnics. Throughout the country, hot dogs were the main food, along with beer and popcorn, sold at baseball games and other sporting events.

By the early 1960s, hot dogs attracted more attention from the government. The U.S. Department of Agriculture was making oversight more stringent and requiring more labeling and documentation to avert contamination and spoilage, which could make consumers ill. The government dictated standards by which hot dogs must be cooked and then chilled prior to shipment, assuring the destruction of harmful bacteria. An emerging technology, vacuum packing, further extended the time that hot dogs and other meat could be stored safely.

In Detroit of the 1950s, as in other cities with professional baseball teams, a local meatpacking company supplied the ballpark with hot dogs from April through September. Vendors roamed the crowds hawking beer, popcorn, and other refreshments, their distinctive shouts as much a part of the game's atmosphere as the crack of a bat or the aroma of cigar smoke.

National brands and long-distance shipping didn't yet exist. The supply contract usually wasn't a big moneymaker for the local meatpacker because the team left town for away games ten to fifteen times a season, games were rained out, and often the hot dogs had to be returned or thrown out due to spoilage.

The Detroit Tigers baseball club, always on the lookout to improve business operations and financial performance, noticed in the mid-1950s that hot dog sales were unexplainably weak. The team's management, including Jim Campbell, who would become team president in 1974, decided in 1956 it could improve hot dog sales by changing the method of heating and presenting them. Until then vendors lugged buckets or cases of hot water which kept pre-cooked hot dogs warm. Roller grills such as those used in movie theaters, seemed to produce a more appetizing hot dog for customers who were willing to get out of their seats. But the hot dog the Tigers were selling seemed to wilt and fall apart when heated on a grill. Managers at the stadium noticed that lots of hot dogs, half eaten, were showing up in the trash.

Campbell determined to resolve why fans at Tiger Stadium found its hot dogs unappetizing and do something about it. The Tigers executive launched a search for a new supplier.

When word reached Hygrade that a search was on for a new hot dog supplier to Tiger Stadium, Hygrade president Hugo Slotkin got excited. Slotkin was convinced the company could gain much prestige by selling the company's hot dogs to Tigers fans. The contract wasn't likely to be a big moneymaker; in fact, it was sure to be an operational headache, with returned meat from the stadium every time the team finished playing a home stand. Slotkin asked his Wurstmacher, Gus Hauff, to create a tasty hot dog that would hold up well on the stadium grills.

Hauff got to work. He had been hired years earlier during a taxi ride in New York City by Slotkin's father Sam, the company's founder. Hygrade managers set up a grill at its Michigan Avenue plant to test Hauff's new concoction.

One in particular proved quite tasty to Hygrade managers and maintained its shape during the cooking process. More importantly, Campbell and Tigers' management liked the way Hauff's hot dog tasted and looked. They awarded Hygrade the contract.

The positive impact on sales at Tiger Stadium was immediate. Hauff had added veal to the recipe to create a meatier, tastier hot dog. The company decided to make them larger as well. Instead of the usual ten hot dogs to a pound, Hygrade's hot dogs would be eight to a pound.

Winning the Tiger Stadium contract happened at a time when hot dogs were a problematic business for meatpackers. The supermarkets were selling the item as a loss leader to consumers, which meant rock-bottom prices for little profit or even a loss, in order to attract shoppers into the stores. Consequently, supermarkets were engaging in price wars, haggling with meatpackers over as little as a penny a pound. The spiral downward was demoralizing for the meat industry. Hygrade, which had spent much time and effort improving the product, was in a quandary.

Sometime in 1958 or 1959, Hugo Slotkin called a Saturday meeting at Hygrade's plant on Michigan Avenue to brainstorm a response to the sickly pricing of hot dogs. Charles Bellamy, Hauff, and other managers from the plant attended. In the midst of the discussion, someone suggested that Hygrade should respond to the destructive price war by creating a premium product, a "better" hot dog than the ones that were being sold as loss leaders and that, consequently, contained the cheapest ingredients.

But maybe—just maybe—supermarket shoppers might pay a premium for a tastier hot dog. Slotkin and his confederates knew that baseball fans at Tiger Stadium were fans of Hygrade's premium hot dogs sold there.

Assuming the grocery chains would be willing to consider such a product, what would it be called?

"How about Ball Park Franks?" came a suggestion from Bill Willtsie. He was a well-liked Hygrade salesman and longtime Detroiter who had landed with Allied forces on D-day and come to work for Slotkin after the war.

Why not "Ball Park Franks?"

If supermarkets could be persuaded to buy a premium hot dog, it would have to be demonstrably better than the ones currently being sold, perhaps like the ones at the stadium. Once more, Hauff's creative powers were summoned.

Once more, Hauff tinkered with the recipe and added veal, creating a duplicate, or nearly so, of the product sold at Tiger Stadium. Hygrade spent a small fortune sending salesmen to conduct taste tests in the supermarkets' meat departments. The shoppers seemed to be impressed. In subsequent months, Hygrade spent another small fortune distributing samples of Ballpark Franks to shoppers in order to promote the idea that a better-tasting hot dog at a higher price was worth the money.

The strategy worked. Hygrade continued to sell the supermarkets and grocery stores cheaper hot dogs under its own name as a loss leader, as well as the more profitable Ballpark Franks, which increasingly were perceived as more pleasing and of higher quality. The supermarkets, which almost always featured the food in newspaper advertisement, responded by affording Ballpark Franks advantageous placement in their refrigerated display cases.

Hygrade copyrighted the names "Ballpark Franks," "Stadium Franks," and lots of other variations to create a tie-in with sporting venues and to protect its intellectual property.

A brand was born. Much work remained and a few decades would go by before we fully understood how valuable the name Ballpark Franks was and how central to the company's future it would be.

CHAPTER 6

Ball Park Marketing

By the time I took over as Michigan sales manager in 1963, consumers throughout the region were searching for Ball Park Franks at their supermarkets and paying premium prices for them.

We had much going for us: Tigers fans at the stadium and in supermarkets displayed their affection for Ball Park Franks by buying more and more of them, despite the higher price we dared to charge for a premium hot dog. Sportscasters from other cities often would mention during radio broadcasts that Tiger Stadium had "the best hot dogs in the world."

The brand definitely showed it had legs outside the stadium as Farmer Jack, Chatham, A&P, Kroger, and many other supermarket chains were ordering our brand. For the first time, we were spending the money to unleash a regional advertising program, supervised by our advertising agency, the W. B. Doner & Co. Fortunately, Hygrade brass was smart enough to reinforce the product and urge more people to try it.

Shortly after my appointment as Michigan sales manager, I was directed to bring my sales staff to a big Hygrade sales meeting at Carl's Chop House in Detroit. Carl's was a top restaurant and bar where the well-known executives running the auto industry and other personalities about town went to see and be seen. The reason for the meeting was to introduce Sonny Eliot, whom Hugo Slotkin had hired to promote Ball Park Franks and other Hygrade products.

I had no idea that I would be called upon to introduce Eliot and run the meeting. Luckily, such impromptu speaking assignments didn't throw me.

Eliot, the magnetic and popular TV weatherman for Detroit's NBC affiliate, became a powerful weapon in our arsenal. Television was a relatively new phenomenon in the 1950s and usually took itself quite seriously. Hence weather-reporting tended to be sober and scientific. The host of the eleven o'clock weather forecast had gained a lot of attention because he was a natural, lighthearted comic, dispensing jokes that today would seem corny. ("It's 82 degrees in Miami, where businessmen lie on the beach—about how much money they make.")

Born Marvin Schlossberg, Eliot was well-liked, highly credible and extremely effective in his role as pitchman. He was a war hero, who was shot down over Europe in a B-24 and survived in German captivity. Everyone in Detroit had stories about his generosity and their affection for him when he died in 2012 at the age of ninety-one. If he said Ball Park Franks were delicious, that meant a lot.

Eliot exemplified the budding practice of using television celebrities to endorse products in the mass media. Meatpackers of Hygrade's size and stature hadn't been accustomed to spending large amounts of money on advertising to support products. But the dollars devoted to the marketing of hot dogs, when spent wisely, expanded unit volume and market share to the extent that we could see rather plainly its beneficial effect on the bottom line. It didn't take us long to figure out that we should start testing markets adjoining Detroit and outstate Michigan.

Toledo was the first experiment to validate our theory; before long, Ball Park Franks became a market leader in northern Ohio. The feeling of excitement and enthusiasm caused by the brand's acceptance outside Detroit was palpable inside Hygrade. Company profits were gaining strength, as was my stock with senior management.

Yet Hygrade's balance sheet was never as strong as we—or the shareholders—thought it should be. We weren't close to realizing our sales potential, which meant we had to enlarge our market and the area in which we did business. Advertising had ignited hot dog sales in the Detroit area and as far as Toledo, based largely on the Tigers and the opportunity for consumers to enjoy the same hot dogs they could buy at the stadium.

Hugo Slotkin, though he loved our association with the Tigers, wasn't so crazy about the large sums it cost Hygrade to sponsor radio broadcasts. After listening to him complain, I determined to see what might be done to negotiate a better arrangement. I telephoned the main number of the Tigers and asked to speak to the person responsible for the team's advertising.

The operator connected me to Neal "Doc" Fenkell, the team's director of publicity. After explaining who I was, we agreed to meet at Carl's Chop

House, not far from the stadium. I explained that Hygrade cherished its association with the baseball team. The cost was onerous, I explained. Could he think of a solution, I asked?

Fenkell immediately offered to reduce the overall sponsorship to an on-air mention of Ball Park Franks during pitching changes. The cost was a small fraction of what we had been paying. We shook on it.

The meeting with Fenkell was the start of a long friendship. He often came to our house for barbeques. I sent him on Hygrade-sponsored speaking tours to tell baseball stories and, of course, to plug our hot dogs.

On the heels of our experience with Sonny Eliot in Detroit, we asked W. B. Doner to create comparable programs in other cities. Finding local radio or TV personalities in other cities wasn't difficult—the bigger challenge was inventing a stirring slogan or message, a call to action, that would be effective everywhere. Given our experience with Ball Park Franks, we used the West Virginia brand on hams, which wasn't nearly as effective.

The meat business of the 1960s was dominated by huge national corporations, which included Oscar Mayer, Hormel, Armour, Swift, and Hygrade. They all had two things in common: first, their names were used on dozens and dozens of meat products from liverwurst to bologna to kielbasa. Second, they had been around for decades without much tinkering to their identity. Local meat companies and brands, like Ball Park Franks, had begun using modern marketing techniques to attract new groups of consumers and carve a niche. In the fall of 1965, we asked W. B. Doner to consider if, together, we could find a strategy to project Ball Park into national prominence.

My contacts at Doner were eager to the task. But they wanted to understand the product better, what defined it, what made hot dogs a special eating experience and, most importantly, why consumers would pay more for Ball Park Franks than those of our competitors. Only then could the agency's creative minds craft the proper language and images for an effective campaign. Doner encouraged me to interview any and all workers at the plant who really knew hot dogs and keep my ears open for an angle or message that might emerge from our conversations.

The Hygrade worker who unquestionably possessed the most "local knowledge" was Gus Hauff, the company's Wurstmacher who came up with the formula that won over the Tigers in 1957. This new assignment wasn't about tinkering with a new sausage recipe. Trying to elicit marketing ideas from an old-school sausage maker was no picnic. Of German descent, Hauff was stocky, outspoken, and temperamental. On his best days I might have described him as "gruff," as he navigated the hams and rump roasts in a blood-spattered smock, barking orders to his minions. We valued his skills, because he was one of the best sausage men in the business, proven during his thirty-year run with the company. We were convinced, without a doubt, that he knew everything there was to know about Ball Park Franks.

Hauff and I talked. The ad agency executives, I decided, were better off hearing what he had to say with their own ears. I tried, with difficulty, to imagine how such a meeting might unfold: the Wurstmacher was at home amid frozen carcasses and meat cleavers. How could I send him to W. B. Doner's marble-and-glass headquarters in Southfield to meet the account team and creative talent, many of whom would be dressed in thousand-dollar suits? I set up the meeting, sorry that I couldn't sell tickets to what promised to be a memorable cross-cultural dialogue.

As all of us hunkered down for the discussion, which took place at our plant, one after another of the copywriters posed the question: "What makes Ball Park Franks so special?"

Hauff squirmed uncomfortably, gathering his thoughts. "Well," he said, "we use only fresh beef trimmings and pork picnics in our formulation." ("Picnic" is a term referring to a pig's foreleg and shoulder.)

Not hearing a million-dollar jingle in Hauff's answer, an art director tried again. "Why should someone pay extra for these hot dogs versus the competition?"

The Wurstmacher pondered the question. His annoyance growing, he tapped his fingers on the glass table. "I added veal to make the emulsion leaner," he said. No award-winning campaign in that answer either.

One of the account executives tried a different tack. "Why did the Tigers pick this hot dog over the dozen others they tested?" Finally, the sausage maker heard a very precise question that could be answered with Germanic specificity: "Because they plump when you cook them."

Flashing lights! Ringing bells! A slogan, finally. They plump when you cook them! The hot dogs the Tigers had been serving tended to shrivel when they were heated at the stadium, Hauff explained, making them unappetizing. His recipe, using leaner trimmings, held up better when the hot dogs were heated; in fact, they plumped when you cooked them.

Hauff's statement embodied all the makings of a perfect advertising campaign. Research showed that the characteristic "plumping" of Ball Park Franks when cooked made them more appealing to consumers than competitive products. And, happily, the process could be demonstrated graphically on film in a thirty-second commercial.

Finding usable footage from all the film of hot dogs on the grill turned out to be anything but simple in the days before computers. Lots of attempts, including one that required ten thousand hot dogs, yielded a few short, very effective sequences that showed how our hot dog got plumper, which we used again and again for years.

The commercial featured two cartoon characters. One asked the other, "What plumps when you cook them?"

The second responded, "Popcorn? Cake?"

"Nope," the questioner replied, "Hot dogs!" And then "Ball Park Franks—made with only the finest meats, lean beef, juicy pork, and tender veal. They plump when you cook them."

Once the commercial began airing on local television, Ball Park Franks's share of the Detroit retail hot dog market expanded dramatically, doubling in a very short time. It would be impossible to overestimate the importance of an impactful commercial and memorable slogan backed by a great product.

CHAPTER 7

Meat Goes Modern

An obvious fact about hot dogs and all other meats is that they're perishable. Despite advances in refrigerated transportation and vacuum packing, meat had to be shipped from plants to retailers and made available to consumers as quickly as possible. The quicker the meat arrived at stores, the more time it could remain on shelves, with less loss due to spoilage.

After World War II and through the 1970s, a plant's distribution radius mostly defined its customer base. Each plant was staffed with its own sales force of men and, increasingly, women who called on grocery stores and chains to promote and sell the plant's products. Meat had to arrive as fresh as possible and sales personnel had to be able to call on customers by driving no more than a few hours, a day at the outside.

As refrigeration and packing technology improved, the market of each plant grew larger, the sales personnel drove farther, and the competition among meatpackers grew heated as their territories overlapped.

The place where consumers bought meat was changing along with trends in distribution and marketing. An old-fashioned grocery store relied on the merchant to fetch from the shelf what the buyer wanted. Self-service became common as stores grew larger. The first true supermarket was opened in New York in 1930. But as people moved from cities to the suburbs and began to own automobiles, neighborhood grocery stores gave way to regional—and later, national—supermarket chains, with large parking lots. A&P and Kroger were the first truly national supermarket chains. In Detroit, we had Food Fair, Farmer Jack, Great Scott!, Chatham, Big Bear, Wrigley's, and others.

The retail grocery business operated on extremely low profit margins. With larger scale, the big chains could negotiate better terms from wholesalers, using that advantage to shave pennies off the price of many items. Thus big chains with lower prices could attract housewives who pored over the newspaper advertisements to comparison shop. The chains also were always able to sell a few popular items at breakeven or at a loss, to attract shoppers—hot dogs were among the most common of these so-called loss leaders. Smaller stores, with less selection and negotiating clout, couldn't compete and eventually vanished.

In the 1960s, Ball Park Franks manufactured at Hygrade's new modern plant in Livonia, Michigan, were gaining recognition and popularity all over Michigan and Ohio and even further through the Midwest. We decided to introduce the brand into more national markets. Chicago, Tacoma, and Philadelphia were obvious choices, because we operated plants in those cities.

Chicago was the home and the fortress of Oscar Mayer, No. 1 in the nation and our biggest competitor. It was the first company to focus exclusively on processed meat products. Oscar Mayer—later to be sold to General Foods and eventually to Kraft Foods—didn't manufacture a particularly delicious hot dog, but the company had done an excellent job with consistency and branding. Wherever Oscar Mayer was sold, it tasted the same. Its jingles and TV spots were memorable.

We made a gutsy decision by challenging Oscar Mayer on its home turf. Thankfully, we won over customers and progressed steadily, soon rising to the number-two spot. Philadelphia was a trickier venture, because the East Coast was dominated by "all-beef" hot dog brands, such as Nathan's in New York. Our hot dog, by contrast, was a formulation of beef, pork, and veal.

I envisioned Ball Park Franks as a national brand, and no brand could conquer the nation, in my view, without first conquering New York. Philadelphia would be our base camp from which Hygrade would push to the top of Mt. Everest, that is, New York. Before bringing our production to Broadway, we had to see how it played in Philadelphia.

As an up-and-coming executive, I knew that big goals require planning, discipline, and perseverance. It didn't matter whether in business or in personal life, these were the principles that led to accomplishment. Shortly after my fortieth birthday, I walked into the Hughes & Hatcher men's clothing store to buy a new suit. The salesperson handed me a size 46— several sizes larger than what I had been wearing for years. Truth be told, I was heavier than I'd ever been. I handed the suit back to the salesman, determined to lose thirty pounds before buying another suit. Three months later, after a strict diet and lots of exercise, the extra weight was gone—nothing fancy, just the discipline of less food and more movement. Many of life's goals are simple to achieve with the right amount of determination and single-minded purpose.

To compete on the East Coast we simply had to develop a premium all-beef version of Ball Park Franks, and, of course, Gus Hauff was the man for the job. A native New Yorker, he learned his craft there, formulating all-beef hamburgers and Franks. Developing a premium, all-beef Ball Park Frank turned out to be a piece of cake for him. We brought it out in the spring of 1966, with promising initial sales.

I couldn't help imagining what it would be like to extend the brand even further. I began to wonder whether our thriving hot dog business was a strong sub-brand of Hygrade's lunchmeat, ham and bacon enterprise—or perhaps a brand unto itself, that could stand on its own anywhere in the United States?

In 1967, Hygrade promoted me from sales manager to general manager of Michigan operations and the Livonia plant, extending my authority over manufacturing and distribution, as well as sales and marketing. The announcement was made at the company's annual management meeting. Charles Bellamy was called to the podium to make the announcement.

Everyone smiled and congratulated me. Hugo Slotkin also announced that his sister, Selma Ross, had decided to sell her stake in the company. I had lunched with her occasionally, at her invitation, a meeting I guessed was meant to provide her with another view of how her family's business was doing. None of us could imagine what had happened behind the scenes to prompt her to sell her stock, but anyone could see that a family member selling out added much uncertainty to Hygrade's future.

Shortly after transferring me to Michigan from Indiana, Hugo Slotkin had singled me out, letting me know that I would rise in the company over the course of my career as long as I fulfilled the potential I was showing. In those days, I guess he wasn't thinking about a change in control of his company. The added scope of my responsibilities and the mysterious sale of Selma Ross's stock weighed on my mind as I traveled to Cleveland to attend the 1968 annual convention of the Super Market Institute, later to become the Food Marketing Institute.

Jim August, our account executive at W. B. Doner, was scheduled to receive an award for a television commercial that the agency had created on behalf of Food Fair, a Midwestern chain. August had come to the meeting accompanied by his colleague, Skip Roberts, who was a vice president of the agency.

The three of us went out to lunch, at which time I got to know Roberts. He definitely knew the grocery business, quoting statistics and names left and right. He dressed sharply, knew how to order wine, and was cultured. I was impressed. I absorbed a great deal about marketing in the grocery industry at the convention and at lunch with the agency men.

A few days later, August surprised me with a call to say he was leaving W. B. Doner. He had decided to fulfill a lifelong dream of going out on his own to start a small agency.

"I wish you well, Jim," I told him. He assured me not to worry, that W. B. Doner would shortly name a new manager for the Hygrade account.

"No need," I said. "I've just chosen one."

"You have?" was his baffled response.

"Skip Roberts," I said. The dapper agency executive from W. B. Doner had impressed me a lot during our lunch, so I decided on the spot to entrust Hygrade's business to him.

"Clyde, that's great that you're recommending Skip, I think he would be a fine choice, but Doner's senior management will want to decide," he said.

"Jim, don't worry, they'll choose Skip." A week later, Roberts was announced as the new executive in charge of the account.

Technically, the selection of an account executive had been the prerogative of Doner's top executives. As a practical matter, an important client such as Hygrade always had the most to say about who would represent the agency and certainly could veto anyone it deemed unsatisfactory. I regarded the Ball Park brand as my baby. The judgment call had to be mine, because I would be spending a lot of time with Skip and he clearly was best suited to be our partner in taking the brand to the next level.

By deciding on my own, I probably was stretching the boundaries of my authority. I was thrilled and excited to be embarking on a new adventure with Skip, strategizing with him how to make Ball Park Franks a household name all over the United States.

Hygrade was selling a first-class premium hot dog alongside the less costly hot dogs that had been its stock-in-trade. My goal and the message to my sales staff was to convince the grocery stores and supermarkets that we were selling the best hot dogs and the cheapest hot dogs—they needed those, and nothing in between.

In 1968, fate intruded with a more consequential matter that didn't have an immediate effect on me, though it soon would: Hygrade was up for sale.

Chapter 8

Newton Glekel Comes to Detroit

The news that an investor was amassing Hygrade common stock in what looked like a hostile takeover of the company startled me, though it shouldn't have. Hygrade's bottom line, despite the success of its hot dog business, was weak. The price of its stock reflected its mediocre financial performance and its cloudy future.

The meatpacking industry of the late 1960s was crowded with ambitious companies that were able to post respectable profits, big names like Armour and Swift. Stronger balance sheets afforded them more and cheaper credit to finance operations and more cash to invest in expansion, acquisitions, and new technology. Though I never was fortunate enough to study for an academic degree, I knew from a lifetime of experience starting on the farm and later in a slaughterhouse, that business ultimately was a Darwinian process: those companies that adapted best to a constantly changing environment survived; the rest were toast.

The industry was consolidating into a number of large national enterprises as the viability of regional companies diminished. Brands clearly were growing in importance, while the opposite was true for manufacturing plants that weren't in highly advantageous locations. The Slotkins weren't intimidated by the changes in meatpacking, but convincing the outside world of their staying power was more difficult after the sale of stock by Selma Ross, Hugo Slotkin's sister.

Hygrade's weak stock price was a red flag waved at Wall Street's bulls. The best plan, Hugo Slotkin decided, was to hang tough, to keep reinforcing the Ball Park brand, and to prepare for the possibility that his family might have to sell its stock.

As the Slotkins feared, an acquisitive investor shortly materialized in the person of Newton Glekel, a shrewd financier from New York whose previous knowledge of meat extended no further than his dinner plate. Glekel had earned a reputation in the 1950s as a moneyman and dealmaker. One of his forays had been to buy the failing Indiana school bus maker, Wayne Works, Inc., on the theory that Supreme Court decisions requiring bussing to achieve racial equality would prove financially beneficial to the company. His biggest triumph, which temporarily made him a darling of the investment community, was purchasing control of the A. S. Beck Shoe chain. Reorganized from a shoe chain into a conglomerate called Beck Industries, its shares rose by the end of 1968 to nearly $160 each from a low of $20.

Glekel, then fifty-four, a graduate of Williams College who was educated and trained in the law, had parlayed his family's money as the seed capital to pursue leveraged buyouts—a financing technique, usually dependent on easy credit, that used the assets of an acquisition target for the borrowing of additional funds needed to buy out the target's owners.

He used a different technique to gain control of Hygrade. Hygrade's common stock, traded on the American exchange, had been languishing in the neighborhood of $20 a share, a depressed price that reflected the company's poor financial performance. A leading analyst in the food industry termed it "a sick company," having posted a net loss of $4 million the previous year. Fresh from his triumph at Beck, Glekel bought 20 percent of Hygrade's stock, paying prices that averaged roughly $50 a share. Other investors, hoping for an outcome similar to his reorganization at A. S. Beck, bid the shares up to $83. Glekel discussed all kinds of plans, including the possibility of acquiring a restaurant chain. No wonder Selma Ross—and other family holders unsure of the company's business prospects—were inclined to sell. Hugo Slotkin reportedly wanted to fight Glekel, but others in his family weren't inclined to borrow the large amounts of money such a fight could have cost. Hygrade's board decided to name Glekel, who had become the company's biggest shareholder, acting CEO, and chairman of the executive committee.

Glekel suddenly was in charge of a company of whose business he knew nothing. A chauvinistic New Yorker, he believed in the superior wisdom of anyone from his city over anyone living to the west or south of the Hudson River. Accordingly, he immediately hired Heidrick &

Struggles, the management recruiting firm to replace many of Hygrade's top executives as part of a management restructuring.

After first hinting that Hugo Slotkin and other family members could remain with the company, he did an about-face and forced them out, including Hugo, within a few months. Glekel began to install Ivy League-educated executives, mostly from the east and many of whom had little or no experience with perishable goods.

I met with Glekel for the first time in the spring of 1969 at the Livonia plant, my general manager's authority rather fresh and untested. His entourage toured the factory as I explained the operations and answered questions. A week or so later, we met again at the company's first management meeting. As managers watched, a newly hired controller, a newcomer named Groom, filled a blackboard full of figures. He seemed particularly interested in numbers relating to the respective average selling prices of Ball Park Franks at the Livonia, Philadelphia, and Chicago plants.

The lowest average price was attributed to my plant, Livonia. I understood right away that new owner correctly identified Ball Park Franks as the company's cash cow, its most important moneymaker. Second, I realized that Groom's analysis was flawed. At first glance, hot dogs manufactured at the Livonia plant didn't look nearly as profitable as those from Chicago or Philadelphia. But Groom's analysis was incomplete: without the corresponding sales and cost numbers they obscured some important facts. Livonia was the only one of the three plants to be selling significant tonnage, and critically, its sales revenue was supporting the retail advertising needed to dominate the category. Livonia's discount pricing and heavy advertising strategy stood in contrast to Hygrade's everyday pricing and small market share elsewhere.

During the break, I politely suggested to Glekel that he may wish for the controller to recap the average profitability by plant, alongside the corresponding sales numbers and other relevant data that had been omitted.

"Clyde here called my attention to additional facts, and I can see why," Glekel said, after the break. The numbers I had related taught Glekel an important nuance of the hot dog business, telling a much different story than Groom's. I was reminded that, as a prudent executive, I would have to protect my flank, no less among peers than competitors.

A few days after the first management powwow under new ownership, I received a phone call from New York.

"Clyde, it's Newt. Please call me the next time you're in the city on business," he said. "I'd like to get together and meet." He mentioned that I should expect periodic phone calls from him to discuss business.

As previous supervisors had done, Glekel had put an asterisk next to my name, designating me one of his key subordinates at Hygrade. He could see that, unlike many of his new hires, I actually understood the meat business in fine detail. Another significant relationship in my business career seemed about to take flight. The mentorships had started with Dan Cassidy in Dothan and had included Thomas Sinclair at Kingan, and, later, with Hugo Slotkin and Charles Bellamy at Hygrade; they were initiated because at key moments I identified and could explain metrics and facts to my superiors that were critical to the business's success.

A few months into his tenure as Hygrade's owner, Glekel began to get a feel for operations and people. He still hadn't found a president and, clearly, had no intention to keep running Hygrade himself, a job for which he would have been profoundly unqualified. After considering a few Hygrade executives for promotion, he gave the job to management recruiters at Heidrick & Struggles.

In 1969, following much sifting and interviewing of dozens of candidates, Gerald Roche of Heidrick & Struggles presented Dick Berg, forty-five, to the board of directors. Berg was serving as executive vice president of John Morrell & Co., a meatpacker founded in Iowa and later sold to United Brands in Cincinnati. Berg told the *Wall Street Journal* in a published interview that he'd always wanted to run his own company. He came highly recommended as smart, virtuous, and personable. Berg indeed was attractive, well-spoken, and could quickly analyze business problems. He had the additional virtue of having worked for Hygrade early in his career on the West Coast, so he knew the company as well as the industry.

Berg's salary was set at $80,000, with the chance to earn up to $40,000 more in bonuses and a healthy bundle of stock options—a hefty pay day in 1969 dollars and double what he'd been earning at Morrell. For finding Berg, Heidrick & Struggles earned a fee of $25,000, according to the newspaper account.

Prior to hiring Berg, Glekel had invited me to meet him during one of his periodic visits to the plant. I was a bit shocked and flattered when he offered me the position of general sales manager for the entire company, a coveted and prominent post that would take me out of day-to-day operations, away from the factory floor.

My immediate concern was with whom I would be working among Hygrade's many new executive hires. "You'll be reporting to Jerry W.," Glekel said, referring to an executive recently recruited from a Texas food company to be Hygrade's vice president of marketing. My heart sank. I'd already been in a few meetings with Jerry W. and had a chance to see him in action. He impressed me as someone who was in over his head and struggling.

"Thanks for the opportunity, Mr. Glekel," I replied, "but I'd be grateful if you'd keep me in my present station as general manager of the Livonia plant."

Glekel looked surprised and a little confused. "Why, Clyde? This will be a great opportunity for you."

I thanked him and expressed my appreciation for the offer. He pressed me, asking why I wouldn't accept the promotion.

"Mr. Glekel, I don't think Mr. W. is a good fit in his current position, and I can ill afford to put myself or the company at risk by accepting a position that my superior isn't qualified to supervise."

My statement was frank, perhaps too much so. I wasn't sure how Glekel would respond.

He hesitated for a moment, then said, "Until I can review the situation further, you will report to me directly as Hygrade's general sales manager. Done?"

I extended my hand and said, "Mr. Glekel, you've got your man."

Truth be told, I believe that Glekel finally offered me the job of managing sales for the company because he hadn't been successful recruiting an experienced sales executive from another meat company. Of course, I was working under the supervision of Berg as well, but Glekel made sure to stay in touch with me and keep tabs on what was happening at Hygrade.

Newton Glekel, the polished and educated New York financier and I, the Alabama farm boy with a wealth of on-the-job training, would go on to forge a special working relationship over nearly two decades. First, I had to perform as sales manager, of course, which afforded me much responsibility and allowed him to remain more or less hands-off. Brought up in an East Coast world of sharp elbows and coarse speech, he seemed gratified by my habit of showing respect and deference to elders and superiors, which derived from my Southern upbringing.

Within a couple of years of our handshake, his dependence on me grew. He rapidly promoted me to vice president of sales, then to vice president of sales and marketing and, finally, to executive vice president.

Years later, Glekel's nephew told me that Glekel's association with me was the closest he had with anyone in his career, a comment that I appreciated without being able to judge how true it was.

CHAPTER 9

Hot dogs Go National

Dick Berg, Hygrade's president, told me in 1972 that Glekel had instructed him to close the company's money-losing plant in Tacoma, Washington. The hog-slaughtering facility had been built in the early 1900s, making it the company's oldest and least technologically sophisticated. It produced a full line of packaged meats, including hams, bacon, and, starting in 1970, Ball Park Franks.

I understood clearly why Glekel, a cold-eyed financial man, was determined to close the plant. But I also knew that Tacoma, the only plant that Hygrade operated west of the Mississippi, could be critical to our future. If we were going to achieve the goal of turning Ball Park Franks into a national brand we needed a plant that could distribute product efficiently to consumers in the western United States.

"Newt," Berg told me he said to Glekel, "Why don't you give Clyde a chance? Maybe he can straighten out the place."

I viewed Tacoma as an opportunity. Glekel already had decided to shut the plant down. If I didn't succeed, Glekel would turn out to be right, a few months' time the only thing lost. If I could improve performance significantly, however, suddenly Hygrade would be in position to operate an efficient, profitable distribution center in the West, one that could further strengthen the company's national aspirations for a branded hot dog business. The brain trust agreed to give me six months. I didn't realize at the time that the episode in Tacoma was more than an opportunity for Hygrade; it was a chance to show my ingenuity in a completely different way, one that would strengthen my leadership position in the company.

For some time, long before Glekel realized it, I had known that Tacoma was running far below its potential. The main problem was a lack of discipline with regard to meeting production goals, keeping sales commitments, and achieving quality standards. Profit margins in the highly competitive business of selling packaged meat were extremely thin, so a "near miss" or an "almost" often meant having to post a loss for a week or a month or a quarter. Poor discipline, or just about any serious problem at a manufacturing plant, almost always can be a traced to a single root cause: weak management.

Since Tacoma was now my baby, I decided to fire Al W., the plant's general manager, a move that should have been made long ago. Next, I began to review the credentials of Frank Kirk, an industry executive of whom I had heard from my contacts. I was getting around more as executive vice president and made sure to pay close attention when anyone, especially a competitor, bragged about a rising star or complained about an underachiever.

Kirk had been running Farmland Meats in Kansas City, Missouri, having learned the business in the employ of Swift & Co. Prior to his business career he had been a U.S. Navy carrier pilot. In my brief stint in the navy, I had learned that the military, and particularly such high-precision specialties like carrier aviation, demanded a special brand of discipline and created a singular breed of warrior.

At my invitation, Kirk and I agreed to meet at American Airlines' Admirals Club in Chicago's O'Hare airport, where we conducted a lengthy interview. Based on our one conversation, his background, reputation, experience, and credentials, I offered him the job of running the Tacoma plant.

Naturally, near the end of our interview he asked about pay. I was conversant with industry pay scales and what he had been earning at Farmland. I told him, "Let's not tussle over salary. If you do a good job you'll get more money than you thought possible. If you don't, you won't be here."

Evidently, my bluntness didn't deter him. He understood my meaning. We shook hands. In short order, he set to the task of fixing the plant.

Kirk turned out to be a tough disciplinarian and a perfect antidote for what ailed Tacoma. Just as on an aircraft carrier, where planes were taking off and landing and being fueled, the equipment and machinery in a meat-processing plant always had to be spotless and in perfect working order. No one could be late—or early on the job, lest safety be compromised.

Carelessness wasn't tolerated. It didn't matter whether the weather was bad or the seas were rough.

Whether landing planes or shipping hams, quality had to be damn near perfect. Kirk called a meeting of key personnel each morning at seven to taste and critique hot dogs, hams, and bacon; nothing short of excellence was acceptable. Employee theft of meat products had been suspected as one of the reasons the plant wasn't meeting its production or financial goals. Kirk instituted a Draconian inspection policy. Every vehicle leaving the plant, including his own, was subject to search. He made sure everyone saw that the trunk of his car was opened and his vehicle thoroughly examined.

A fair number of the workers and managers objected openly to the military style that Kirk introduced. Soon they were looking for new jobs. Others, who figured out that improved quality and productivity actually helped safeguard their job security, won promotions under the new regime. I flew out to Tacoma several times during Kirk's first months. The mood and demeanor of the plant were noticeably upbeat. An atmosphere of pride had replaced the grousing over discipline and the embarrassment caused by the anti-pilfering measures.

According to performance parameters, Hygrade's plant in Tacoma had risen to the company average, on a par with the others. I was pleased. But Kirk kept pushing. As a result, the plant's numbers kept improving. At the end of his first year on the job I sent Kirk, as promised, a fat bonus check. Soon thereafter, he became a company vice president.

With Tacoma now humming, my plans to increase hot dog sales on a national basis had gotten a big lift. Because the plant and the machinery were so old, they had been fully depreciated. Had we not been able to improve performance, the dilapidated plant would have closed, the machines sold for scrap. But now, with a highly skilled and motivated workforce in place, new investment in state-of-the-art hot dog manufacturing equipment could be justified. The outside of the plant remained pretty rough looking, but inside, the manufacturing process had been brought up to date. We were ready to expand hot dog sales in the West, a campaign that would entail risks much bigger than those we took to fix the plant.

As I looked more deeply into Hygrade's operating metrics, the Ball Park Frank brand struck me more and more as a key—maybe *the* key—to the company's long-term profitability and its very survival. Sure, economic growth and the popularity of hot dogs as a cheap and easy means of feeding a family were important. But I also could see plainly how much more enthusiastically consumers reacted to a product with a brand that resonated—and how much more they would yield in revenue—compared to a product that was faceless or generic, that failed to denote specialness or excitement.

During my adult life, the way that nearly everything was sold had changed radically. Building brands became the job of marketers and advertisers via the mass media. Due to the invention and rising popularity of television, radio, and the movies, mass media and the brands they were selling influenced which products sold in greater volume and at higher prices. How did Kleenex sell so much more tissue, and at a higher price, than generic brands? Why was Coke the leading soft drink? Tissue and sugar water didn't have many attributes that distinguished one product from another. Clever advertising had become a psychological tool, more or less hypnotizing consumers so that they grabbed for brand names with a predictability that would have impressed Pavlov.

Hot dogs were no exception. A hot dog brand had to establish a relationship between a consumer and the product. First, the advertiser established awareness. Next, the advertiser educated shoppers about what the brand promised to deliver. The promise had to be convincing in order to stimulate a purchase. The product had to deliver so that a second, third, and fourth purchase would take place. "They plump when you cook them" was an effective promise, one that was easily adapted to advertising and one that delivered a delicious hot dog. And with Skip Roberts at the helm of our account at W. B. Doner & Co., I felt confident that our relationship with consumers was growing stronger.

My association with Roberts and the Doner agency opened my eyes to many nuances in the successful marketing of a food product. One was the role of packaging. Grocery store items often were purchased impulsively, the decisive factor being the product's appearance, whether the deep red of a tomato or the twinkle in the eye of the tiger on a cereal box. In the case of meat, vegetables, and other fresh foods, consumers wanted to see what they were buying.

Hot dogs, because of their pale color, didn't look especially appetizing when packaged in transparent cellophane. To compensate for their bland hue, the meat industry often employed red crosshatching on cellophane to make the meat look pinker. It was a clever disguise, one that annoyed the regulators at just the wrong time.

The federal government in the late 1960s and early 1970s was a hotbed of regulatory activism, with mandates for new water-and-sewer treatment plants, automotive safety equipment, and myriad other requirements covering all sorts of commercial activities, including the packaging of processed foods. As we were considering how to expand distribution of Ball Park Franks beyond the markets defined by the plants in which they were produced, the United States Department of Agriculture invoked regulations banning crosshatching on meat packages, asserting that they falsely conveyed an image of freshness that might be inaccurate. If packages used transparent material, at least 50 percent of the entire package had to be transparent.

We weren't sure whether to continue packaging our hot dogs in clear cellophane or to change our approach altogether. We decided to analyze the question carefully, knowing that hot dogs often were an impulse buy, chosen because of their appearance as they lay in the refrigerated display cases. Skip Roberts, savvy advertising executive that he was, recognized that first-class package design was a specialized expertise, one that Doner didn't possess in-house. He recommended hiring a New York-based package design firm that had achieved beneficial results for several Doner clients.

Bud Jarrin and his firm Jarrin Design were based in New York, though he had many Michigan connections. He had studied at the Pratt School of Design and worked for the legendary Harley Earl, design director of General Motors. Several U.S. government agencies hired him to create international exhibitions. Later he was employed as a consultant to a number of companies including RCA, Campbell Soup, and Mattel. Roberts had gotten to know Jarrin when he was recruited to restyle the logo and packaging of Faygo soft drinks, a Detroit-based client of Doner's.

Jarrin flew out to meet us at Hygrade headquarters, his physical appearance very much in keeping with the stereotype of an offbeat, creative personality: wispy hair, ill-fitting suit, multicolored tie. We sat down to discuss the nature of what faced us: we had to develop a new package under the stricter federal guidelines; it had to be compelling, else we could be forced to use entirely transparent material to display our hot dogs so their true color was visible.

I hired Jarrin and sent him back to New York to get started on the project. A short time later, on a trip to Manhattan, I dropped by for a visit and to gauge progress. The guy had taste and style, evident from his Porsche sports car and the flair with which he ordered expensive food and wine at fancy restaurants. His studio consisted of the bottom two floors of a brownstone on the Upper East Side, every room crammed with bold, geometric art. I was immediately struck by how much each of his pieces demanded attention, forcing me to look and examine and reflect. I only hoped that our new hot dog packaging would do the same.

A few weeks later the big moment arrived when Jarrin showed up at our office with a dozen possible designs. He saved the best for last, an entirely opaque package with a black background. A photograph of a delicious looking grilled hot dog appeared ready to eat, creating the effect of a magazine ad for each customer shopping among the brands. This very pleasing design contradicted that conventional wisdom that consumers insisted on viewing what fresh foods they're buying. They wouldn't see the hot dogs until they opened the package, and we prayed it didn't matter.

The logo was new. The words "Ball" and "Park" were in bright yellow, stacked on top of one another, a little pennant waving from the second L, obviously a sly reference to a championship sports team. The reaction of the Hygrade and Doner executives to Jarrin's creation was unanimous and enthusiastic: brilliant.

All of us at Hygrade—and Doner—were feeling nervously ebullient. Our advertising campaign and new packaging now were aligned, as well as the physical capability to manufacture and ship hot dogs and other meat products in several major markets. One activity remained a worry though: sales.

The meat business's traditional model, with each manufacturing plant employing its own staff to sell primarily the products produced in that plant, rapidly was becoming obsolete. We were having trouble justifying the cost of employing salespeople by the volume and pricing of meat the plants were selling. We needed somehow, through higher revenue or lower cost, to generate more free cash to invest in advertising. It had dawned on me with great impact that the promotion of our products through the mass media was becoming a critical ingredient for increasing market share and strengthening prices.

I'd noticed that a few meatpackers deliberately broke with convention, relying on brokers rather than on an internal sales force. Brokers called on whomever they wished based on where they had the best chance to be successful. They lived from the commissions they earned from the meat they sold at wholesale. They didn't take possession of the meat; rather they made arrangements for shipment from packinghouses to stores. Brokers worked independently; they weren't exclusive and could represent whatever products they wished. I had always been skeptical of them, for it seemed to me they were like consultants: having failed in paid sales jobs, they put out a shingle and called themselves brokers.

I've rarely been more wrong about anything.

My change of heart could be traced to the day when Dick Berg, early in his tenure as Hygrade's president, asked me to join him for lunch and meet a food broker who was visiting Hygrade. The broker was David Freedheim. The lunch meeting was inauspicious, partly due to my inherent bias against brokers, based on my belief that they were ineffective. I didn't attach any particular importance to the broker's visit.

Freedheim, on the other hand, struck me as an exceptionally intelligent and personable individual, with great knowledge of the food industry. The son of a corporate lawyer from Cleveland, he had graduated from Bowling Green University and then, after a stint in the army, had earned a master's degree in business administration from Harvard Business School. He learned food retailing at Kroger, left the company, and relocated to the West Coast, where he started a brokerage, selling cheeses and other perishable food products at wholesale to grocery chains.

A few years went by. I didn't hear from Freedheim or anything about him. I had plunged deeply in my role as vice president of sales, trying all sorts of tactics to improve the performance of the company's salaried staff to grow revenue. Hygrade's mediocre revenue performance, leading to poor financial results, had become a constant worry.

Our formerly underachieving Tacoma plant on the West Coast was rebounding remarkably under new leadership. Following Kirk's arrival, I began to look at the West Coast as an area of great potential, a market where our products were in a relatively weak position in the big grocery chains like Safeway, Lucky, and Alpha Beta. On a trip to the West, I called on one of our salesman in San Francisco, Joe Rickart, to hear an assessment and solicit ideas for increasing sales, especially for our hot dogs.

Rickart's response astonished me. He proceeded to tell me about an extremely able San Francisco-based broker by the name of Freedheim, whom he thought I should meet immediately.

It couldn't be anyone but the same fellow who had visited us a few years earlier. Freedheim lived in a fancy house in Sausalito "with a big mortgage," Rickart explained, implying that the broker was very motivated to increase his income. As for Rickart, he said he was amenable to leaving the employ of Hygrade immediately provided I agreed that he could work for Freedheim instead. I'd never heard such a thing from one of our salespeople. He was willing to show Freedheim the basics of the hot dog business and get him up to speed quickly with Ball Park Franks.

Obviously, Rickart saw more earnings potential in working for Freedheim than for Hygrade. His startling suggestion forced me to reconsider more deeply my inclination against brokers and think the matter over more carefully. For some time I had been disappointed with the output of our sales staff. Suddenly, I was hearing a company salesman say he was certain he could be more productive in a different system. Perhaps a divine or cosmic plan was unfolding. I made an appointment to visit Freedheim.

Rickart's suggestion and the meeting with Freedheim happened at a fortuitous moment. ABC television was beginning to offer extremely low rates for national advertising contracts. Hygrade had a chance to extend its reach into more markets, places it hadn't had a presence, but it wouldn't work unless we could add brokers to our sales force.

Over lunch at Tommy Toy's, a Chinese restaurant in the city, I decided to offer Freedheim the opportunity to represent Hygrade as our first broker. The man obviously was knowledgeable about selling perishable foods to retailers and seemed to know everyone who was important in grocery chains on the West Coast. The risk of hiring his brokerage, Kay-D Company, was minimal. We agreed on a commission, which struck me as reasonable, for all the meat he could sell. I agreed to pay him weekly, an unusual practice in an industry that usually paid commissions once a month.

Freedheim exuded confidence, assuring me that he could introduce Hygrade products into Safeway and the other West Coast chains. There was no long-term obligation from either party. If he failed to produce he wouldn't be around long. If he couldn't make money with our products, he'd drop us. To mark the occasion, we sketched out our agreement, including his promise to meet a certain sales quota, on the back of a napkin.

With our salesmen reporting to the Tacoma plant, Hygrade had been selling a reasonable quantity of meat in northern California. Freedheim committed to increase that number fivefold once he got rolling. Our agreement included Hygrade paying a special incentive, a doubling of our normal discount, if he could also convince grocers to sell Hygrade brand hot dogs along with premium Ball Park Franks. Years later, we still referred to our agreement as "the Chinese Covenant."

Freedheim was enthusiastic about associating with Hygrade because he knew the Ball Park Franks brand in particular could improve his business and attract other accounts. I confessed to him my longtime reservations about brokers being little more than glorified consultants.

He didn't seem a bit insulted. A born salesman, he pulled this one from his bag of jokes. "You know what a consultant is, don't you?"

"No," I replied.

"A consultant is a guy who knows a hundred different ways to make love—but doesn't know any women." I laughed. He struck me as a congenial fellow who probably knew many ways to make love. I hoped he also knew a lot of women.

The switch to using Freedheim as our broker on the West Coast and away from company sales personnel inevitably reduced the authority of our plant manager in Tacoma, to whom the sales staff had reported directly. Kirk wasn't happy about losing control over the sales. He would just have to accept, like all of us, that changes in business force everyone to adjust.

I was communicating directly with Freedheim and, together, we dreamt up promotions for our products. Another agreement he and I hatched, this time at the Tadich Grill seafood restaurant in downtown San Francisco, and likewise written down on a napkin—we called it the "Tadich Treaty"—specifying how much I would be spending on television advertising to promote our hot dogs, as well as how much Freedheim promised to sell. I told him to monitor competitive prices in the newspaper and call me at home on Sundays, that I would set his pricing as well as what we spent on "allowances," i.e. discounts.

I heard from Freedheim that Kirk, whom I held responsible for the profitability of his plant, was disappointed to be losing his grip over sales strategy. Freedheim had no illusions about who was setting his agenda and knew that I was holding him responsible for the performance of our products.

Freedheim, as promised, managed to gain the agreement of the major chains to carry Hygrade products. I wondered if our new broker was really as well-connected as he claimed. To test his stories, I conducted an experiment by asking him to get me invited to tour one of Safeway's meat-processing plants, a favor the supermarket chain didn't grant easily. The plant was one of Safeway's newest; I wanted to see it. He accomplished the mission right away. In all respects, he was exceeding expectations.

With our advertisements introducing Hygrade's premium hot dog brand to the public by way of television commercials on local TV stations, Ball Park Franks in a matter of months rocketed the company to No. 1 in the category for the Bay Area and northern California. Armour had been the leader, followed by Oscar Mayer, which was spending very little on advertising. I can only imagine their managers scratching their heads and wondering how they had been knocked from the leadership perch so abruptly.

Our success on the West Coast, with a broker selling our meats and the savings gained by not employing a sales staff, suggested a powerful new model for improving our financial results. We used our cost savings to advertise more heavily, which in turn pushed retail sales higher. Hot dogs in particular represented a growth category beyond anything we had seen. We identified the seventeen "magic weeks" between Memorial Day and Labor Day as a peak period of barbeques and celebrations that drove the sales of hot dogs. If supermarkets were willing to commit up-front to large orders, we were willing to reduce their price via bigger discounts. No one hustled the holidays like we did.

On one Fourth of July weekend, when lots of special events and backyard barbeques would be taking place, we decided to extend special discounts to grocers for particularly large orders. As a result, we sold an enormous quantity of meat that week, an eye-popping total beyond anything we had dreamed possible. I immediately began wondering about what a sharp broker could do in southern California. I also began to analyze Hygrade's other markets, with an eye toward hiring more brokers and spending more on advertising, especially in big population centers, where our flourishing hot dog brand would benefit.

CHAPTER 10

Top Rung of the Ladder

As Hygrade's executive vice president and No. 2 executive to Dick Berg, I was constantly traveling around the country to processing plants, to Washington for regulatory and trade conferences, to meetings of the American Meat Institute and to New York and other major cities to supervise sales and marketing campaigns. My business career was flourishing, though the price in terms of my personal life was heavy. Looking back, I wish I had had more time at home. I believed then, as I do today, that a man's primary duty is to provide a living for his family. I didn't know how to do that in any other manner or level of intensity than the way that I did.

I knew that my presence was missed at home, and certainly my attention was devoted mostly to Hygrade rather than to the day-to-day details of school, hobbies and events around the house. I'll never forget one evening, Pat and I were attending a discussion on current events led by a prominent Detroit Free Press columnist, Judd Arnett.

A young girl, maybe sixteen, stood up to speak. After she had spoken I said to Pat, "That girl was remarkable. Very bright and articulate." She looked at me. "You have one like that at home," referring to our teenage daughter, Margaret. I got the message.

Margaret and our son David mostly grew up in Redford, Michigan, where we chose to live when I was transferred to Detroit from Indianapolis. Margaret played the clarinet and belonged to the marching band. David was interested in technical subjects pertaining to radio, television, and electronics. Often, business meetings at the plant or with clients kept me busy until late, which meant I arrived home after the children went to sleep.

If there was a recital or special event, I always tried to rearrange my schedule in order to attend. On Saturday nights, typically, I cooked steaks outdoors for the family on our barbeque, highball in hand. Pat prepared the salad and potatoes. We enjoyed the meal together as a family.

My wife didn't complain about my absences when duty called. The second-highest job at Hygrade demanded a great deal of time and energy. But she knew how to get my attention when the family needed it. She reminded me, gently, when I was missing too many experiences a father should be able to enjoy with his children.

***

The meat industry operated more or less like a club. Its members, the companies and their executives, were cordial most of the time, always keeping an alert eye on what products and marketing strategies the others were trying. The top executives at companies and retailers got to know one another at industry meetings and through the American Meat Institute, its main trade association.

I had been representing Hygrade at meetings since the 1960s. As I got to know more and more people in the industry, my activities on behalf of Hygrade during the mid-1970s drew the attention of other companies that were seeking fresh blood for their executive ranks, including new presidents. I suppose I had won the respect of my peers and their bosses, because I began getting calls from headhunters to gauge my interest in moving to another company. I heard from Morrell, Rath, and others, my name included on short lists of finalists.

I was flattered, naturally, but I didn't discuss these approaches with Berg or Glekel, since they might have viewed them unfavorably. As I saw the matter, they might have interpreted my report of entreaties as a way to gain a promotion or an increase in salary. As a matter of fact, I wasn't interested at all in leaving Hygrade to run another company. I enjoyed the expanded scope of my responsibilities as executive vice president, which allowed me use the knowledge and experience accumulated over thirty years with a single company. Hygrade had been good to me. I had started in Dothan with the most menial work, weighing hogs, and progressed many levels to the most sophisticated and intellectually challenging puzzles of how to use mass media and advertising and how to exploit price disparities and create more profit from our sales.

Nevertheless, Glekel somehow found out about the job feelers from competitors and confronted me. There weren't too many secrets in the meat industry, probably not too many in any industry. I reassured him that I wasn't unsatisfied and that I wasn't looking to jump ship.

The calls from headhunters kept coming; they were upsetting and making Glekel uneasy. He relied on me. He knew that Berg was the symbolic leader of the company and respected by everyone, but other key executives, especially me, were doing the heavy lifting. Berg hadn't made major mistakes or botched anything. Glekel could plainly see that executives around him were taking the initiative on all key matters.

Though extremely intelligent and well-liked, Berg belonged to a category of chief executive that wasn't particularly tough or engaged when it came to enacting policies or introducing solutions, especially if they disrupted the status quo. When it came to rocking the boat, others had to step in. The rise of Ball Park Franks more and more proved that our business was reliant on a few products, which meant we needed strong leadership to devise new tactics and strategies. We had to take a fresh look at many processes and systems. Reforming or eliminating them often was painful.

For the time being, Hygrade's executive team was effective and worked well together. We could have kept managing Hygrade that way, except Glekel grew nervous—despite my reassurances—that I finally might respond to one of the headhunters to run another meatpacking company. He knew he'd be stuck in that event because Berg wouldn't be able to get much done on his own. Glekel, having considered the situation, confided in me in 1975 that he'd decided to ease Berg out and promote me to president.

I told him it wasn't necessary, that he could put Berg in charge of government relations and let him carry on with the president's title. The rest of us would keep doing our jobs, running Hygrade and responding to the changing industry. Glekel appreciated my willingness to put the good of the company ahead of any ambitions; he also said it wasn't fair to me. No, he had decided; he was moving Berg out and putting me into his job.

Glekel's decision hit Berg like a bolt out of the blue. At first the news didn't seem to sink in. I knew this because Glekel called me after he had briefed Berg about the decision, telling me "the deed was done." Shortly afterward, I saw Berg and was amazed that he didn't say or indicate that anything unusual had happened. I called Glekel and told him that Berg wasn't letting on that anything had happened. Perhaps he was in denial. Finally, Berg acknowledged his termination. He asked Glekel to give him some time to find another job. In short order, he announced he was accepting a post as a senior executive with Wilson meat company in Oklahoma City.

In what seemed like the blink of an eye, I realized that the entire responsibility and authority for Hygrade's success—its existence and survival—rested on my shoulders. It had been a long journey from the wooden shack where I had been born to the president's office at headquarters.

Along with Berg's office, I inherited his executive assistant, Amy Canter. She had worked for Hugo Slotkin prior to Berg's arrival. Like many assistants to top executives, Canter was one of the stealth assets of the corporation. Efficient, pleasant, dependable, and humble, she performed her duties with a great sense of professional purpose, usually undertaking critical tasks and duties before she was asked.

We became a great team. Amy had an uncanny sense of what to say and, more importantly, what to omit. Often she would field calls from colleagues or family members wanting to know where I was. I had no reason to withhold that information, but she would habitually reply, "I'll ask Mr. Riley get back to you as soon as possible." Every noon she would take a walk, not just for exercise. She was scrupulous to avoid fraternizing with other secretaries and assistants, lest she inadvertently reveal a sensitive piece of information at one of the gossip sessions.

On September 12, 1975, the *Wall Street Journal* announced my promotion, at age forty-eight, to the presidency of Hygrade. I wondered if many of the readers of that newspaper remembered the glowing front-page profile of Dick Berg a few years earlier. The gist of the article had been that Berg represented a new breed of American business executive. Traditionally, executives were groomed for top posts from within the company's ranks. This new type of chief executive, epitomized by Berg, hopped from company to company, rising along the way in authority and responsibility. Berg indeed had started at Hygrade, moved to Morrell, and then returned as president to Hygrade. But Hygrade reverted to tradition with my promotion, awarding the internal candidate—me!—the top job thirty years after I had joined the company.

The small story in the *Wall Street Journal* publicizing my promotion omitted a few facts that were important to me, namely that I belonged to a very small number of chief executives of U.S. public corporations who had never had the benefit of a college degree, that I was the first in my family to graduate from high school and that I had started working for my company at the very bottom, in the most humble job imaginable, and climbed to the very top.

If the newspaper had seen fit to publish a more extensive story, I'm sure I would have explained to the writer that I regarded my promotion—in fact, my entire career to that point—as a resounding testimonial to my family, to my teachers, mentors, and to my colleagues, all of whom had provided me with so much opportunity: I had started life on a small farm, with few obvious advantages beyond the guidance and support of my home and school. Yet I'd been allowed to travel far and to achieve much. Everywhere I went, people seemed to reach out to help me at every juncture. I've never seen or heard of anyone else with such good fortune.

****

I'd barely grown accustomed to my new title and responsibilities as president when Hygrade and its shareholders were surprised in late 1975 by the interest of a potential acquirer from Great Britain, Hanson Trust Ltd.

During Glekel's seven years as chairman, Hygrade had managed to grow a bit in sales and earnings, though nothing like the stock market anticipated when he first took over. The share price, which had briefly quadrupled during the excitement of a new owner, settled back to where it had been under the Slotkins and barely budged. The flatlining of Hygrade's stock price was bound to cause trouble eventually, attracting a bargain hunter with capital that could wring better results from the company and thereby force the company's value higher.

That someone turned out to be the English industrialist, Sir James Hanson. Hanson, a lifelong supporter of Great Britain's Conservative Party, had been successful in a variety of businesses, starting with oil. He was a handsome, suave presence who had served as an officer in World War II in the Duke of Wellington's regiment and had been engaged briefly to the actress Audrey Hepburn. Through the 1960s and 1970s, he mastered the technique of identifying undervalued companies, buying strategic stakes and then reorganizing them or sitting pat and benefiting from cash flow. Because he was ruthless about selling or closing underperforming operations, critics accused him of "stripping" assets, a charge he vigorously rebutted.

Glekel called me one day late in 1975 when I was in New York, after a U.S. subsidiary of the Hanson Trust disclosed that it was buying and amassing Hygrade shares.

"Come on over to Twenty-One for lunch," Glekel said. "Someone wants to meet you."

Sitting at the center of a long table, flanked by subordinates, was

Sir James. He greeted me cordially. After a few pleasantries, he posed a deceptively simple and straightforward question, "How do you manage Hygrade?"

Fortunately, I had anticipated this and was ready. I was accustomed to answering such pointed and direct questions, having spent my career making sure I always possessed the data and facts to back my assertions. More than an hour later, Sir James gestured that he had heard enough.

"Please bring the finest bottle of wine you have," he commanded a waiter. He looked pleased with what he had heard. Evidently, I had passed his test.

"Don't change a thing," he told me.

Hanson had begun buying Hygrade common shares a few months earlier at roughly $28 each. A group of minority shareholders thought the price wasn't sufficient and sued. Within a few months, Hanson bumped the price to $30, the litigation was settled, and Hygrade recommended that all the holders tender their stock to the new English owners of the company. The entire company had cost Hanson roughly $30 million.

Sir James, whose financial interests spanned a broad spectrum of industries, kept Glekel in place as chairman and me as president in charge of all operations. Sir James knew as little as Glekel about the meat industry and the ways it was changing. Hanson was less interested in growing the enterprise than cultivating Hygrade as a dependable source of cash: as long as the company performed from a financial perspective, Sir James, and therefore Glekel, were likely to be satisfied.

After the acquisition, Hanson was the only shareholder. Glekel remained my direct supervisor and gave me complete authority to run the company, a fact that conferred operating latitude and ensured that my leadership duties wouldn't be unnecessarily complicated with politics or issues of control.

CHAPTER 11

Nation's Favorite Hot dog

I'd led and directed Ball Park Franks' evolution into Hygrade's bread-and-butter product. It remained so under Hanson ownership, a big moneymaker that flew off shelves wherever we sold it. The meat formulation was richer and costlier than ordinary hot dogs, which made it more expensive to produce and much tastier. The key was to keep reminding and convincing shoppers they were worth a premium price, which we accomplished by a clever combination of advertising, promotion, and package design.

The nation's strongest single brand remained Oscar Mayer. Oscar Mayer, a meatpacker started by German immigrants, developed a very powerful name that translated into high consumer awareness of the "Oscar Mayer wiener," which was heavily advertised on television and radio and supported by a catchy jingle. Skilled use of media made Oscar Mayer the No. 1 seller, starting in the 1960s. Oscar Mayer's wieners were easily identifiable in refrigerator cases by the distinctive yellow bands on the packages. Back in 1936, the company built and displayed an Oscar Mayer "Wienermobile," a vehicle that looked like a hot dog and toured fairs and other spots to generate consumer interest. Nathan's Famous and Sabrett's also were strong hot dog brands in New York and on the East Coast but without the broad national appeal of Oscar Mayer.

A brand wasn't just a name under which we sold our product; it was a valuable asset requiring protection. Our brand could be strengthened, extended, copied, disparaged, damaged, or even destroyed, and it always was at risk.

We found out just how much risk in October 1982 when our precious crown jewel tumbled alarmingly into harm's way. The trouble started the day the police in Redford, a suburb adjacent to Detroit, fielded an odd complaint that a woman had found a razor blade in a Ball Park hot dog she'd bought at her local supermarket. She'd asked for a free bag of groceries, which the manager of the store refused to give her. No one had called us. We learned about the incident on the Channel 7 news in Detroit after a reporter responded to a tip.

We were distressed, of course, though we weren't quite sure what we were dealing with. How could a razor blade have found its way into one of our hot dogs? Could a disgruntled employee have put it there in one of our plants? Had some lunatic tampered with a package at the supermarket? We talked to workers at our Livonia plant, looked everywhere, and didn't find anything obviously amiss. We scrutinized our manufacturing system again and again to determine whether we were missing something.

Current events provided a clue. Earlier the same month, the nation had been stunned after seven people in Chicago died of cyanide poisoning due to contaminated Tylenol pills, which were manufactured by Johnson & Johnson. Investigators concluded that the packages had been tampered with in stores, not in Johnson & Johnson plants. The public was in a justifiable panic; and the pharmaceutical giant was in mortal danger of losing its most important product unless it dealt with the crisis swiftly and effectively.

Though the Tylenol tampering had evidently taken place at the retailer where the pills were sold, Johnson & Johnson swung into action on a number of fronts. Tylenol was recalled from shelves. A tamper-proof bottle was developed swiftly to meet an evolving set of federal standards. In short order, the health-care products company addressed the calamity forthrightly, setting a standard for other companies in similar situations. Had it not acted expeditiously, I believe the pharmaceutical giant could have been crippled or put out of business.

Product tampering suddenly was front and center in the public consciousness. Could the Tylenol episode have inspired others to terrorize, attack, or extort Hygrade?

With the Tylenol episode fresh in our mind, we knew we had to reassure our customers and distributors, while getting to the bottom of what was going on. And we knew we didn't have much time. Once doubts about Ball Park Franks entered the mind of consumers, it would be just as easy for consumers to skip ours and begin to buy Oscar Mayer or another company's hot dogs. Likewise, supermarkets weren't about to stock their shelves with a suspect food.

I happened to be in New York on business when the Channel 7 report was broadcast. Brod Doner, chairman of our advertising agency, called to suggest strongly that I engage the services of Jack Miller, a shrewd lawyer and one of the founders of the Detroit law firm of Honigman, Miller, Schwartz and Cohn. Miller in turn suggested we hire Wylie Cossar, an experienced detective he knew, to investigate and gather facts: we worried that we had only a short time to answer many questions and to reassure the public before our brand might be damaged and beyond redemption. Police agencies tried to be helpful, but they had many priorities and couldn't find answers as fast as we needed them.

The first item on our agenda was recalling all our hot dogs on grocer's shelves, hundreds of thousands of pounds of meat in five Midwestern states including Michigan. The meat had to be packed and shipped back to our plants for inspection. To ensure that no tampering had taken place, we bought metal detectors so workers at our Livonia plant could examine the packages for tampering. Our employees were eager to do whatever was needed. They volunteered to stay late and to come in on the weekend so the extra tasks could be accomplished with a minimum of disruption to our business. As soon as the hot dog packages were examined and determined to be unopened and free of razor blades or any other foreign material, we repacked and shipped them back to grocers and supermarkets.

Cossar, our detective, tried to question the woman who supposedly discovered the razor blade. She was a resident of Detroit who claimed she had bought the hot dogs at a Farmer Jack supermarket in Redford. Her husband, an officer for the Detroit Police Department, refused to allow his wife to talk to us or clear herself with a polygraph test. Though it was impossible to get to the bottom of where the razor blade came from without facts, we strongly suspected the woman had inserted the razor blade with the intention of asking the supermarket for a free bag of free groceries, which is what she did. But the supermarket refused to go along, so she turned to Channel 7, which was only too happy to broadcast her story.

Unfortunately, the original TV report of the so-called tampering led directly to more trouble for us. Following the broadcast, consumers reported more than a dozen incidents of razor blades, pins, and other foreign matter in Ball Park Franks. We suspected these were "copycats." A few of the complainants may have been attracted by the idea of a television news truck arriving at their home. Our detective and local police departments looked into every incident; not a single one turned out to be legitimate.

We had to conclude these were imitators, looking for publicity, attention, or just money.

Ensuring that the public knew Ball Park Franks were safe was critical to saving our brand. We hired Beverly Beltaire, a Detroit-based public relations specialist to advise us. I designated Charles Ledgerwood, our vice president of operations, as the spokesman for the company. Ledgerwood, a charming and affable man, convened a press conference to answer reporters' questions and explained, as much as possible, how we were responding. Murray Feldman, a reporter with Channel 2, WJBK-TV called to say he'd like to do a story about how the workers were involved in the effort to examine our product and to ensure that the meat was safe to eat. Ed McNamara, who was mayor of Livonia and later would become Wayne County executive, presided over "Livonia Loves Hygrade" week, a publicity stunt designed to boost morale that featured a hot dog roast at city hall.

In short order, as more stories were publicized raising doubts that any hot dogs had ever been unsafe, life returned to normal. A negative story had been turned into a positive, as we showed what lengths we would go to assure our customers' safety. Ball Park Franks returned to grocery shelves, and consumers resumed buying them. Our brand, Hygrade's crown jewel, weathered the storm. The Public Relations Society of America the following year awarded our company a Silver Anvil for "getting Hygrade off the griddle." The episode cost us more than $1 million, but it could have been a much bigger catastrophe.

Oddly, I believe our company was much stronger as a result of the way we responded to the tampering. The value of the company and the Ball Park Franks brand increased because we showed consumers that we would go to any length to protect them.

An epilogue to the story unfolded during discussions with Michigan legislative representatives in Washington, DC about how to prevent and deter product tampering. Sadly, we had learned that people committed such acts because they were deranged or pathologically in need of attention. Revenge and extortion also were motives. Incredibly, no federal law existed that established precise grounds for prosecuting a person found to be committing the heinous act of tampering with a product in way that could harm a consumer. The law changed in 1983 when the U.S. Congress passed the Federal Anti-Tampering Act.

Hygrade had dodged a bullet, as had Tylenol. As a result, the public would be safer in the future.

CHAPTER 12

Everyday Headaches

Managing the crisis over razor blades brought home to me just what an enormous responsibility rested on the shoulders of any enterprise's chief executive. Virtually every decision that the leader of a company made had to be correct. If the decisions were easy, then a subordinate ought to have been making them.

The job of running a big corporation looked attractive to outsiders and to the rank and file, because it seemed to be all about the pay and perquisites, the big corner office and generous expense account. Very few on the outside could appreciate the daily torrent of difficulties that had to be resolved decisively and with tact, lest the company lurch into peril. A leader's judgment had to be very close to unerring.

During my early tenure as president, I was forced to focus on ways to control costs, not just increase sales. Hanson expected healthy profit and cash flow every quarter. One of the biggest drags on Hygrade's financial performance was the leverage wielded by organized labor over our plants, forcing us to pay noncompetitive wages. We were working under a master contract, which meant that all our plants and locations were covered by one agreement. The handicap to management was overwhelming, because if the workers at any plant were dissatisfied with wages, benefits, or working conditions, they could call a slowdown or a strike, the effects of which would ripple through our system since we needed meat from one plant for a product made at another. We were often at the union's mercy because it had the power to shut down the entire enterprise.

We needed more flexibility than a master union contract permitted. As such, I was constantly on the lookout for an opportunity to free Hygrade of its master contract and negotiate separate contracts at each of our plants. Prevailing wage rates differed depending on the location of the plant, and I wanted to avoid a system-wide shutdown of Hygrade in the event of an impasse at a single plant. It would take time to break free, but I was watching and waiting for the right opportunity.

I decided in 1981 it was time to close the company's Storm Lake, Iowa plant permanently, the location I had been assigned shortly after leaving Dothan. I had a soft spot for the place. As a young manager, I had learned much there about business and life. I made friends and enjoyed a pleasant life in Iowa farm country. In the 1950s, Storm Lake had been highly profitable because it was modern and strategically positioned at the center of the most vibrant hog-producing territory in the United States. Since then, however, the plant became more and more costly to operate for a number of reasons, particularly rising labor costs due to expensive union contracts.

I couldn't afford to be sentimental because of my warm memories of Storm Lake. As president, I faced decisions almost every day that, from a personal point of view, were difficult. The right answers usually were based primarily on what was best for business, in other words, what was best for Hygrade. But I also had to consider less obvious ramifications as well: what message we might be sending to regulators, customers, suppliers, and to our own workforce.

A classic example of a crisis appearing without warning occurred when we received an odd telephone call from a jobber selling meat products. A jobber was a person who bought products and resold them to small retailers. The man, who bought and sold products made by Hygrade competitors, was upset because another jobber selling Hygrade products was undercutting his prices and stealing his customers. The jobber who was complaining noticed that the Hygrade products on retailers' shelves carried a production date marking that was much earlier than it should have been. He demanded to know how his competitor, the Hygrade jobber, could have gotten his hands on our merchandise so early.

Gary Ridgway, who was in charge of the Livonia plant, fielded the call and decided to consult our security officer about what might be happening. He was right: the early production date was odd. The security people wondered if the Hygrade jobber was somehow selling pilfered products. Ridgway, a very sharp executive with excellent instincts, proposed that we install video cameras in the plant over a weekend to monitor what was happening. I concurred.

Sure enough, the tapes revealed that one of the jobbers handling our products, in cahoots with two Hygrade workers in our plant, was loading stolen boxes of meat onto the truck. Presumably, the jobber was able to sell the stolen product to retailers at cut-rate prices since his cost was zero. He then would split the proceeds with the two Hygrade accomplices.

The plot thickened because the jobber's two "inside men" weren't just ordinary Hygrade employees: one was the chief union steward for the Teamsters; the other was the chief union steward for the United Food and Commercial Workers.

Ridgway instantly contacted the Livonia police department, showed officers the tapes, and filed a report. The police told us the evidence was solid, but we'd have to decide whether we wanted to press charges against the jobber and the two union stewards. In the meantime, one of our mechanics accidentally discovered the cameras, and soon all the workers in the plant knew about them. This unearthing of our cameras made the episode awkward for us and, especially so, for the union.

When confronted with the evidence, the jobber confessed. We demanded and received about $10,000 to cover the stolen meat. We decided to fire the two union stewards.

The head of the local Teamsters union paid me a visit to plead for lenience, to keep his two union brothers in their jobs. Truth be told, I was considering reinstatement for the two men out of a sense of mercy and because having them in Hygrade's debt might be useful for the company.

Instead, I turned down the Teamster official's request. I had no choice.

"If these two are allowed to stay," I explained, "my plant manager will quit." Gary Ridgway, by his actions and deeds, had always shown himself to be a fair, decisive no-nonsense leader. He and I communicated very well. (He once told me that if I began giving him instructions on the ninth floor of an elevator ride, he always knew exactly what to do by the time we reached the lobby.) Allowing thieves to remain in their jobs at the plant was unacceptable for Ridgway, and he was far too valuable to lose.

I did exercise some lenience by allowing the two union officials to resign rather than terminate them for cause. The forced exit of the two men came dressed in an object lesson for the rest of the workers: once everyone heard the news, Hygrade's commitment to honesty and integrity was maintained and underscored. I didn't have to worry about losing a key executive.

The episode exemplified Hygrade's approach to leadership, as well as mine. Just as we had discovered during the uproar over the suspected tampering of Ball Park Franks, the response by executives and managers—mine, above all—proved far more consequential than the adverse events that required them.

CHAPTER 13

Taking Hygrade to the Next Level

The years of Hanson's ownership of Hygrade were proving to be the company's best and most satisfying for me in terms of the opportunity I had to lead. I was thankful that the British investment group came along when it did, recognized our value, and put its trust in us and in me. As the company's top corporate officer, I found myself on the guest list of many ceremonial events and was asked to greet lots of dignitaries. At a meat industry conference at The Greenbrier resort in West Virginia, British Prime Minister Margaret Thatcher spoke to our group. Afterward, at our introduction ceremony, I mentioned that we were owned by Sir James Hanson's trust. She appeared delighted to hear his name and exclaimed, "Sir James, he's one of my favorites."

The 1980s was a golden age of transatlantic partnership between Mrs. Thatcher and her counterpart in the United States, Ronald Reagan, whom I had also met. He came to Detroit during his campaign in 1980. As one of his supporters, I had the chance to speak briefly with him. His subsequent election and leadership provided a big lift to the United States, which entered the decade in economic doldrums caused by a global energy crisis. After rampant inflation and the Iran hostage crisis, the country badly needed an optimistic leader who preached individual freedom and responsibility, enterprise, self-reliance, and smaller government.

Those values, which Reagan embodied in spades, rang true with me. I believed in them and still do. Reagan's principles coincided with everything my parents had taught me growing up, with the ideas my teachers preached in school, as well as with the training I received in the navy and from my mentors at Kingan and Hygrade.

The future definitely was looking brighter for the country and for Hygrade on Reagan's watch. Hanson, always wanting to remain informed and feeling expansive about the future, had asked me to submit five-year forecasts for the company. I explained that a prediction so far into the future would prove meaningless, because the meat industry was too volatile. Meat prices were constantly changing, as were consumer tastes. We settled on two-year forecasts.

In response to the food-and-meat industry's fast-changing nature, I could see that the company must not rest in its determination to operate differently than it had under the Slotkins and during Berg's presidency if it was to survive and keep its independence. With constant advances in packaging, technology, regulations, transportation, mass media, and consumer tastes, it was clear that the business model for meatpacking had to become more centralized.

In the past, regional general managers supervising the business of individual packinghouses more or less operated autonomously. They made their own production schedules, pricing, and decided which specific products they would sell in their market area.

As market territories grew larger, neighborhood groceries evolved into giant supermarkets, and the power of brands like Ball Park Franks flourished, it made sense from an efficiency standpoint to create a headquarter-centric strategy for the company. That way, our plant capacity could be used more cost-effectively. For example, we could take advantage of favorable animal prices in specific regions, shipping carcasses or processed meat from one location to another when we could lower costs by doing so.

Moreover, I was beginning to reap the advantages of shrinking our in-house sales staff and hiring more independent brokers—a much less costly and more effective way to sell our products, especially branded processed products like hot dogs and, to a lesser extent, hams.

The division and regional managers, of course, weren't pleased about losing their power and autonomy. As we gave more responsibility and authority to the brokers, the plants were forced to be more responsive to the markets instead of dictating what products they would sell.

Gary Ridgway once more assumed more importance in the company's operational transformation. Charles Ledgerwood, vice president of operations, had promoted Ridgway to manage our Livonia plant. Ledgerwood was a friendly, adaptable type, well-liked by union workers as well as managers, perhaps because he tended toward leniency.

Ridgway's skills would prove invaluable on a number of occasions. He had been hired on as an industrial engineer. A combat veteran in Vietnam, he was rock solid, straight, incorruptible, true, and dependable. You could take anything he said to the bank. I used to tell him, "If I had to escape from a burning building, you're the one I'd want at my side."

In March 1984, Ledgerwood died following a short illness. I spotted Ridgway at the memorial service at Forest Lake Country Club in Bloomfield Hills, where Ledgerwood had been a member. I asked him to take over operations temporarily until we could figure out what to do. As usual, his work and decision-making were exemplary. Shortly afterward, I promoted him to the job permanently.

Ridgway proved to be an able replacement. Previously, he had been instrumental in guiding Hygrade's response to the bogus razor blade uproar. His honesty and integrity were impeccable. I knew I could count on him to lead the broader operational changes that had to take place. I gave him the authority to impose new operating guidelines on our plants in Baltimore, Philadelphia, Chicago, Detroit, and Tacoma. Rather than let them set their own production schedules based on their preferences, he could dictate each plant's schedule based on what products the company at large required, the most favorable costs, when product was needed and where.

Ridgway wasn't much for showiness or ceremony. His predecessor had built himself a fairly plush office behind glass at the Livonia plant. Ridgway preferred a desk in one of the hallways, with a few hooks for hats and coats, which made him more accessible to fellow workers and gave him a better line of sight to all that was happening.

I met with Ridgway and other executives periodically to review orders from our customers and to determine how much we had to produce. During factory-inspection tours, I'd don a white overcoat with my name on it, nodding approvingly, though I wasn't particularly conversant in the specifics of the machinery or the processes.

We'd hold production planning meetings prior to the big hot dog season, which lasted from Memorial Day to Labor Day. Likewise, we'd work out tactics for ham production prior to that meat's two big seasons, Christmas and Easter.

To keep business brisk on the West Coast, I convened a national meeting of four Hygrade divisional managers at Jack's restaurant, one of the oldest in San Francisco. There, over elaborate meals and expensive wine, I fired up the division chiefs with praise and exhortation, encouraging them always to set their goals higher. They, in turn, stood up and promised to sell more meat, to work harder to develop a broader customer base, to do anything and everything to improve Hygrade's financial performance, knowing I would pay generous bonuses when their missions were accomplished. It was an impressive display of loyalty to Hygrade and to me.

After the meeting, David Freedheim and I sat down to discuss our West Coast business. He also had attended the dinner at Jack's, watching and listening as the division managers articulated their promises and commitments for the coming year. Afterward, Freedheim told me he had never seen an executive that commanded so much loyalty or displayed so high a level of personal magnetism and charisma. I was taken aback, because he seemed to be flattering me, which I didn't need. He assured me that wasn't the case, that his observation was genuine. I began to accept the fact that on top of my analytical skills, I'd been endowed with certain innate team-building and leadership qualities that had helped me advance in business and in life. The ability to attract and motivate people, which I hadn't tried to study or cultivate, was a big reason why Dan Cassidy had chosen *me* to help with time-motion studies, that Hugo Slotkin had put *my* name in his little black book, why Newton Glekel had reached down into the management ranks and relied on *my* numbers rather than those from senior executives. James Hanson, after spending millions buying Hygrade, was prepared to turn the company's operations over to *me*, based on a relatively brief presentation in New York. Later on, my peers would nominate me for the highest position in the meat industry's most important trade organization. These weren't coincidences or accidents.

***

As Ridgway and I centralized Hygrade, the company's operations grew more complicated, far beyond what one could control with pencil and paper. We had incorporated computers, relying on mainframes for payroll and other clerical tasks. Personal computers were beginning to take hold in offices and factories in the 1980s for use in other functions such as production scheduling. Ridgway was facile with programs such as Lotus 1-2-3 that could create instant spreadsheets, so I authorized the purchase of an IBM PC for him to work on Hygrade business at home. Who would have dreamed that in a few decades we'd all—even me—be working on personal computers?

But as business operations grew more sophisticated and the business competitive, we remained bogged down by Hygrade's uncompetitive wage structure. In 1985, I summoned Ridgway and our chief financial officer

Rocco Minghine into my office to brainstorm how we might resolve our awful labor contract with the United Food and Commercial Workers union at our Livonia, Michigan plant. The contract was coming up for renewal. The prevailing wage of $10.69 an hour plus benefits was roughly $2 too high in comparison to what other meatpackers were paying in regions that either resisted or had broken the union.

Hygrade had no choice but to extricate itself from pattern bargaining, a concept favored by the union that entailed all plants across a company or an industry being covered under a single labor agreement. The union insisted on a master contract as a way to hold a club over our head by making sure the plants were dependent on one another. If one was shut down due to a strike, the company would be crippled.

Pattern bargaining had given the union too much leverage, in my view. By seizing the initiative and forcing the union to deal with each plant individually, we could keep operating much or most of our capacity in the event of a strike at a single plant.

I told Ridgway and Minghine that I thought Hygrade could continue to operate and survive for a while by paying high, uncompetitive wages and avoiding confrontation. Eventually, though, competitors that figured out how to pay wages that weren't excessive would put us out of business.

I'd be retiring to the happy hunting ground within a few years, I told the two executives. They and younger subordinates would have to face the unpleasant consequences and perhaps might be looking for employment elsewhere.

I was willing to draw a line in the sand, to let workers know that we needed a rational wage structure. We couldn't be sure how the union might react. Were my top lieutenants up for a strike, if events deteriorated to that point? I put the question to them directly: Did they have the stomach for going to the mat with the union and all the stress that would entail? My aim was to "smoke them out," to discover their true level of commitment.

They assured me they were ready for a fight if need be.

Ridgway immediately called on the union to lay out the company's predicament over uncompetitive wages with officers of the local representing our workers in Livonia. As we anticipated, they didn't seem too concerned or sympathetic to management's financial worries.

The officials of the local union explained that Hygrade workers in the plant weren't itching to strike and probably would approve a concessionary contract if they had a chance to vote. Unfortunately, the international union was anxious to stem the nationwide wave of concessionary contracts in the meatpacking industry and had ordered local officials to prevent another one at Hygrade.

Based on a recommendation from Bud Cook, whose family had started Bluebird canned hams in Philadelphia, I hired John Pelino, a very sharp lawyer from Philadelphia, to assist us. Pelino's firm specialized in labor disputes. We had to make sure that we understood what actions we could take and stay within federal labor laws. We girded for battle, determined to buck the tide of history and not accept another bad union contract.

As negotiations unfolded, Hygrade exercised some muscle it didn't have previously. Because we were dealing with a single, albeit critical, plant in the Detroit suburb of Livonia, we could minimize the damage from a strike by stockpiling product ahead of time and by stepping up production at our other plants across the country. We had the option of shipping to important Livonia customers like Farmer Jack and Kroger stores in the Detroit area, over longer distances. Ridgway dispatched some of his managers to Hygrade plants in Tacoma and Philadelphia to prepare them for their role if Livonia workers walked out.

True to their warnings, negotiators in Livonia responded to pressure from the international union and refused to accept any concessions. As soon as the workers' contract expired in early 1986, they walked off the job and began picketing the plant. A few pickets showed up at headquarters as well. My secretary, Amy Canter, called me to suggest that I stay home until the union's atmospherics calmed down.

"They're yelling 'Hygrade's got the gold, and we're in the cold,'" she said in a worried voice, describing the scene from her window.

Ridgway, anticipating trouble, had leased some public warehouse space for storing product shipped in from other cities until it could be sent to local customers. Teamster drivers wouldn't have crossed the picket lines at the plant, but we figured they wouldn't be averse to transporting hams, hot dogs, and other items from the public warehouse, and we were right.

Once the union saw I could move hams to supermarkets, the members showed signs of demoralization. About four weeks into the strike, I could see that everyone had had enough. Picketers were tromping around in cold, snowy weather. They weren't drawing any pay. And to add insult to injury, Hygrade was doing pretty good business and not disappointing customers. The strategy of knocking down pattern bargaining and centralizing operations to maintain flexibility among plants was paying off.

After four weeks of picketing and lots of adverse publicity in the mass media, we decided to advertise in local newspapers for workers to replace the strikers. Hundreds from the Detroit area applied for the jobs. I had to hire big, tough guards to open a safe path among the union picketers so our new hirees could enter the plant.

In short order, Ridgway and his new workers were able to initiate hot dog production—another profoundly demoralizing blow to the union: the strikers now realized they might never return to work if we kept hiring replacements and training them to run the plant.

Six weeks after the contract expiration, we settled, but I was adamant that we weren't backing down from our original offer of a $2 an hour concession. I wasn't about to reward our workforce for going out on strike. And we refused to fire the replacements. We called back striking workers to jobs only as vacancies opened up for them. It was about as thorough a victory as any employer could expect to win.

The sales arm of Hygrade was notching victories too. My decision to hire brokers and employ fewer sales personnel was paying bigger and bigger dividends on the West Coast after the hiring of David Freedheim. Prior to Freedheim, Hygrade products could be found mainly in the smaller supermarket chains, with very little penetration into the big three: Safeway, Lucky, and Alpha Beta.

One by one, Freedheim introduced the big chains to Ball Park Franks. My pricing and revenue strategy was to sell our Hygrade-brand hot dogs as cheaply as possible, the stores relying them as a "loss leader" to draw shoppers. The low-price part of the deal was predicated upon the stores' simultaneous agreement to buy a certain volume of Ball Park Franks, Hygrade's premium product whose price we controlled and which yielded the company a big profit. By the early 1980s, Ball Park Franks went from nowhere, behind Armour and Oscar Mayer, to the No. 1 hot dog in northern California, with nearly a quarter of the market.

As with other brokers I hired, I made it clear to Freedheim that his commitment to Hygrade was actually to me. Personally. I didn't care whom he assigned to the Hygrade account; ultimately, Freedheim was responsible for success or failure. He accepted this commitment, which meant that he and I often huddled, in person or by telephone, to develop tactics for specific accounts or situations that required them.

One day, Freedheim called me to say that Safeway was upset that Alpha Beta was undercutting Safeway's prices on Armour hot dogs, apparently as part of a deal with the rival meat company. Would Hygrade be willing to create and advertise a special price on Ball Park Franks, giving Safeway a retaliatory weapon against Alpha Beta? I told Freedheim to tell Safeway we might agree to drop the advertised price slightly on Ball Park, provided the chain agreed to buy several truckloads of Hygrade hot dogs—for which we would grant a special $3,000 discount per truckload.

Safeway agreed. Freedheim then called, bubbling with joy, to tell me that the chain was ordering seven truckloads of Hygrade, more than 200,000 pounds of product and the single biggest hot dog order we'd ever taken. Because it was my nature to tease Freedheim, especially when he'd accomplished something great, I demanded to know why he hadn't been able sell Safeway *eight* truckloads.

Freedheim, who served as my eyes and ears on the West Coast, monitored the advertising of Hygrade and its rivals carefully, noting which stations and media were most effective. Most of the time we bought newspaper and television ads. We stuck with the catchy slogan, "Ball Park Franks, they plump when you cook 'em," suggested years earlier by our Wurstmacher and developed into a stupendously successful ad campaign by Doner. The mental image coordinated neatly with the attractive picture on the Jarrin-designed package.

Freedheim decided that radio could add an extra dimension to our marketing and flew up to Tacoma to meet me during a visit to our plant there. During a barbeque at Frank Kirk's house, he convinced me to ask Doner to buy some radio ads in the San Francisco market. Doner tended to favor TV over radio, because of the medium's visual power that strongly portrayed Ball Park Frank's "plump when you cook 'em" mantra." I thought the idea was worth a try.

Skip Roberts interviewed a number of radio stations in San Francisco, settling on KPIX, where Wayne Walker, a former football star working as a sports commentator, was designated as pitchman. Our business responded well to the ads, once more reminding me why I had hired Freedheim and Roberts and trusted them so much.

If Ball Park was to become a truly national brand—and I had every intention of making it so—it would have to gain access to the East Coast as well, a market dominated by well-established brands in New York such as Nathan's, Hebrew National, and Sabrett.

Our plant in Philadelphia and its sales staff were responsible for East Coast sales. I could see that Hygrade wasn't doing nearly the job with its salespeople that a broker like Freedheim could—if only I could find such a person in the New York area. Freedheim suggested that I talk to Leonard Epstein—like him, a food broker. Norlen—the name of Epstein's company—had vast experience brokering all kinds of foods that required refrigeration in the New York area.

The opportunity to restructure Hygrade's sales in New York coincided with the death of our sales manager in Philadelphia, Scott Pamploni. I decided it was the right time to make a change and flew to New York to meet Epstein.

Tough, smart, and very businesslike, Epstein possessed the credentials and experience to get the job done. I invited David Freedheim and Skip Roberts to speak with him as well. We all met at Bud Jarrin's house to play pool, discuss business, and get a feel for one another.

I liked what I saw and heard. My instincts had always served me well, so I acted on them without much soul-searching and hired Epstein. Just as with Freedheim, I explained to him that he could appoint whomever he wished to run the Hygrade account but I demanded his personal commitment. In my view, he alone was responsible and I would hold him accountable to me for how well the company's products sold and the satisfaction of our customers, the grocery stores. If I had a problem or a question, he would be hearing from me directly. Likewise, I expected him to call me without hesitation, at home if need be, when the need arose.

The New York grocery market was a dense, bustling place, sprawling over a large area that included the boroughs of the city, northern New Jersey, southern Connecticut, and parts of New York State. Hebrew National and Oscar Mayer were fierce competitors for No. 1 in the hot dog category, with Ball Park a distant No. 3. (Jewish and Muslim consumers on the East Coast often chose Hebrew National because of its kosher designation, which means it contained no pork.) The market was further populated with a bunch of smaller players, including the famous Coney Island hot dog, Nathan's, as well as Sabrett's, sold at pushcarts all over Manhattan.

To add an additional bit of spice to the situation, none other than Newton Glekel, Hygrade's chairman, resided in Manhattan. Glekel, though unlikely to insert himself in a supermarket battle among hot dog brands, occupied a front-row seat to the advertising, promotion, and sales campaigns that Hygrade and Epstein were undertaking on behalf of the Ball Park brand.

Several times a year—sometimes, once a month—I flew to New York to meet Epstein so we could plan promotions prior to the summer hot dog season and the holidays. He picked me up at Newark Airport; we'd have dinner and the next day call on a few heads of supermarket meat departments.

I was the unusual chief executive, in that respect, because the presidents of other meat companies rarely, if ever, met with customers. More than once I flew to the West Coast for a lunch meeting and returned the same day. The meetings were valuable, because they allowed me to cement my relationship with our broker, while teaching me what customers valued, how they viewed our products and giving me an inside track on any scuttlebutt or intelligence they disclosed about rivals or consumers that could be used to Hygrade's advantage.

As had been the case on the West Coast, the power of the Ball Park brand quickly gave Hygrade an edge in structuring combination deals with ShopRite, Pathmark, A&P, and other New York area supermarket chains. With Ball Park as the premium brand and Hygrade as the commodity brand, Epstein was able within two years to push Ball Park past Oscar Mayer and Hebrew National to the No. 1 spot in New York.

The brokerage system was proving itself to be transformative for Hygrade, increasing our profit while building equity in the name Ball Park Franks. I continued to hire more brokers to cover larger and larger territories. As brokers proved more and more consequential to the company's bottom line, I decided to host a big annual celebration for them, usually alternating between Naples and Palm Springs, where we'd celebrate our victories, exchange ideas and best practices, have a few drinks, play golf and tennis, and let our hair down a bit.

I had a hidden agenda for these galas as well. I used every opportunity to recognize and to heap praise on Hygrade's best brokers, lauding them and handing out all kinds of awards. By implication, the underachievers quickly figured out who they were, and if they didn't, I'd let them know explicitly. The party served as a way to say "thanks" to the top performers; it also sent the not-too-subtle message to the slowpokes and underachievers to get their act together or find another line of work.

CHAPTER 14

The Trappings of Office

After serving as Hygrade's president for several years, I received a telephone call one afternoon from Jerry Hiegel, the chairman of Oscar Mayer.

"Clyde," he began, "I'm baffled as to why you've never been called upon by the meat industry to serve as a leader or to be recognized for your contributions. I'd like to correct that oversight by nominating you to the board of the American Meat Institute." He was chairman of the group, the industry's most important trade organization.

The AMI had been founded in 1906 after passage of federal meat inspection legislation in an effort to help companies adjust to the new laws and regulations. I had attended meetings over the years and met many of my peers from rival companies. Our industry had always been collegial. As companies and executives we competed against one another vigorously while remaining cordial and sometimes even friendly. Goff Beach, president of Oscar Mayer, had become aware of me as an up-and-comer and introduced me to Hiegel, who was about to replace him at the company.

"Jerry, that's very kind. I'm probably too old for the job," I told Hiegel, though I knew I wasn't.

"Look, you're a person who has completely changed Hygrade from the type of company it was when you got there," he said. He knew what a task it had been to transform a onetime collection of regional slaughterhouses that sold on price to a more profitable outfit that owned a premium brand.

"The AMI is the kind of place you'll be expected to keep things more or less the way you found them. We have a paid staff that does all the work."

Of course, I was terribly flattered. The appointment was very important personally and professionally, an acknowledgement that I belonged to the handful of people that more or less ran the U.S. meat industry. By accepting a position on the board, I would be placed in line to become an AMI officer. In 1987, I was named secretary, the following year treasurer, and finally, chairman in 1989. As an officer of the group, I would be expected to spend an increasing amount of time in Washington, meeting and discussing industry and other policy issues with congressmen, senators, and on occasion, the president and his advisors.

I felt tremendously honored to be chosen for a leadership position in my industry. It was a mark of respect and affirmation by my peers. It also woke me up a little too, because I realized that this honor was something that happened to an executive toward the end of a career. In other words, I was reminded that the conclusion of my tenure as Hygrade's president was approaching, faster perhaps than I had realized.

I didn't allow my AMI duties in any way distract me from my primary mission of leading Hygrade. Hanson was very pleased and satisfied with its ownership. I had been able to operate the enterprise as a healthy, profitable, cash-generating component of Hanson's diversified worldwide interests. The British company had bought the company during a period of consolidation and specialization in the U.S. meat industry. While I was president, the Ball Park hot dog brand clearly had evolved into the company's most valuable asset and seemed to grow stronger by the weeks and months. Hanson's bet so far had paid off handsomely.

Ideally, Hanson would have preferred to use some of Hygrade's cash to grow the company even larger, probably by acquisition. Hanson's advisers were expert at recognizing value that others had overlooked. My mission included investigating opportunities and using my expertise and connections to determine if Hygrade could buy underperforming meat companies and absorb them on advantageous terms.

Dinner Bell Foods, a regional meat company in Defiance, Ohio, looked to us like a potential target. Ridgway and I drove down to visit the company on a fact-finding mission. We met executives there and toured their plants. It became quickly obvious, however, that few operating efficiencies could be realized by buying the company, and many problems would have to be overcome. In any event, growing Hygrade through acquisition wasn't an idea that particularly motivated me or suited my own preferences for operating and growing the company.

***

When I took over as chairman of the American Meat Institute, the agenda was more or less as it always had been: meat processors were contending with renewed assaults from regulators, legislators, consumer advocates, and unions over inspection procedures, worker safety, and the very wholesomeness of meat. After more than forty years in the business, there were very few of these complaints against the industry that I hadn't heard in one form or another since my days as a slaughterhouse clerk for Kingan in Dothan, Alabama.

From the earliest days of the meat industry, consumers and the media have been quick to suspect that companies were trying to foist spoiled or diseased meat on them and would be successful but for the work of federal inspectors. In truth, Hygrade and any food company that hoped to stay in business had a vested interest, on top of a moral obligation, to take every precaution and spend whatever money or effort was necessary to make sure that consumers bought meat products that were safe and wholesome. Inspectors added another level of safety to what companies would have done in any case.

During my tenure as AMI chairman, the U.S. Department of Agriculture tried to institute what it called an Improved Processing Inspection plan for meat that used modern technology and permitted a reduction in the number of inspectors. Unfortunately, the USDA did a poor job of explaining the new system. Predictably, consumer groups and labor unions got up in arms because it seemed like fewer workers would be carrying out an insufficient number of inspections—a grossly simplistic view that didn't reflect the reality of the safer, better system that was being proposed.

As I said in an interview with AMI magazine in 1989, the public's perception of the new inspection system was poor, because it didn't understand what was being proposed. Perhaps we and the media had explained it poorly. But I promised to work closely with Congress and the USDA to revamp the inspection proposals. I explained that meat companies were more determined than ever to improve worker safety, especially in the field of ergonomics. Meatpacking equipment that had been designed around cost considerations would have to be redesigned to head off all kinds of stress-related and repetitive-motion injuries.

As head of the AMI, I was often asked about the health factors around the consumption of meat, especially beef. Once upon a time, grilling a porterhouse steak over a charcoal fire on Saturday night was a show of status, proving that you'd arrived. Protein was a component of a healthy diet. But because of beef's high status, it was an inviting target for criticism that it contained too much fat and might contribute to heart disease. Chicken and pork largely escaped the criticism, because they hadn't been as exalted as elite foods.

The higher the pendulum swung in one direction, the higher it swung back in the other: as quickly as questions about beef arose, so did efforts to create leaner beef. Soon the medical establishment modified its dire warnings, and in no time diners again were waiting an hour for a table at fancy steakhouses in Chicago and New York.

My twin jobs as president of Hygrade and as top spokesman for the industry made me quite visible and accessible to top executives of the grocery chains, to the media, and to legislators. It wasn't my nature to seek publicity, but I also didn't run for cover when calls came from the press for comment or information.

Fortunately, Newton Glekel had foreseen that I would be in the public eye and prepared me for it. Years earlier, shortly after I'd been named Hygrade president, he invited me to join him at a Democratic Party fundraiser in New York for Jimmy Carter. The election pitted Carter against Gerald Ford, who had come into office to finish the term of the disgraced Richard Nixon.

The fundraiser took place at a fancy Manhattan mansion owned by a donor. The Kennedys were in attendance, as were the Harrimans and other party notables. The first person I spotted and recognized was Bob Strauss, the Washington power broker and chairman of the party. I marched up to him, extended my hand, and introduced myself. Since he was a Texan, I mentioned that Hygrade owned an operation in Fort Worth. Strauss took matters from there and introduced me to many in the room.

Carter, a liberal Democrat who had been the governor of Georgia, addressed the group in his heavy Southern drawl. He talked about the need to "get out in the streets and solve these problems." I suppose he was referring to crime, poverty, and homelessness, topics surely to resonate with New Yorkers. I recall wondering how a fellow like Carter who grew up on a southern farm, as I had, might cope in the hurly-burly of Washington politics. As it turned out, he didn't cope well, which doomed him to a one-term presidency.

Politics interested me, though not as much as entrepreneurship. I read about and was fascinated by John Kluge, a German immigrant who had risen to become the nation's richest individual, according to *Forbes* magazine. Kluge's company was Metromedia. Metromedia's TV stations eventually were sold to News Corp. and became the backbone of Fox TV. His story fascinated me. On an impulse, I mentioned Kluge to Hygrade's broker in the Baltimore area and wondered if a visit was possible. Lo and behold, a short time later he called back to report Kluge would be pleased to meet and show me his estate.

Spread over more than seven thousand acres of Virginia, Kluge's place was opulent beyond belief. He couldn't have been more gracious, introducing me to his wife Patricia, and hosting an entire day of meals and tours of his home, offices, and farm operations. (Patricia, a onetime belly dancer, was Kluge's third wife. He donated his real estate to the University of Virginia in 2001 and died in 2010, at the age of ninety-five.)

At the conclusion of my visit, Kluge suddenly asked whether I was interested in owning Hygrade. The question startled me for a moment. Then I realized that he had the money and could easily finance a management-led buyout of the company from Hanson, with me continuing as the president and part owner. He may have assumed that I came to see him for buyout financing, since a deal of that kind had the potential to make me quite wealthy.

I waved off his suggestion politely. Just as I had never been interested in undertaking an acquisition spree to make Hygrade bigger for Hanson's benefit, I'd also never asked for equity ownership or dreamed of becoming a part owner in order to amass great wealth. What I wanted to do was run Hygrade properly for the benefit of its owners, customers, and employees. That focus on business fundamentals was a blessing, shielding me from distractions that might have ended badly.

***

George Bryan and his older brother John Bryan were among the more pleasant and significant acquaintances in the meat business I'd made as a result of my positions at Hygrade and the AMI. The Bryans, natives of West Point, Mississippi, were a family that had prospered selling meat for a long time. The company had been started by their grandfather and uncle. When I met George, he was a senior executive of Sara Lee, the Chicago-based diversified company that had bought his family's meat business.

"I hear you folks at Hygrade are doing quite a business on the West Coast," Bryan remarked to me one day, apparently referring to Ball Park Franks' astonishing growth in the area after taking over as the No. 1 hot dog brand several years earlier. The achievement certainly had drawn the industry's attention. "I know my older brother John would like to meet you," he said, adding, "I'll tell you now, he's a lot smarter than I am." I took it as a friendly warning.

John Bryan, the chief executive officer of Sara Lee, was a legend in the industry. A personable, brilliant business prodigy, he had been appointed head of his family's $25 million business when he was only twenty-three. John Bryan built up the company and sold it to Consolidated Foods Corp. Less than a decade later, at the age of thirty-eight, he was elected chief executive officer of Consolidated, which had become a big public corporation. Later on, he changed the company's name to Sara Lee, after the name of a famous brand of baked goods that it had bought in the 1950s.

I wasn't quite sure exactly why George Bryan had suggested a meeting with his brother. Once I let him know that I'd be pleased, subsequent events moved pretty quickly. John Bryan called immediately to invite me to visit him in Chicago at Sara Lee headquarters. He was exceptionally cordial and spent a great deal of time explaining the company to me. It had been founded by a Canadian, Nathan Cummings, and owned a portfolio of consumer goods brands, some in foods such as its namesake, which was famous for its coffee cake.

A few weeks later in the spring of 1988, John Bryan called to ask if I would accept an invitation to spend a few days with him at elite Augusta National, the golf club in Georgia where he was a member. Augusta had just been the host, as it was every April, to The Master's golf tournament. The winner had that year had been the Scotsman, Sandy Lyle.

I received word that Sara Lee's jet would be picking me up in Detroit to join John, George, and Jimmy Dean, the country-and Western singer, for a few days of golf, talking shop, and relaxation. Jimmy Dean, on top of his music career, had founded a company whose main product was a pork sausage. His company was later bought by Consolidated Foods and became a successful brand under Sara Lee's management, trading on his fame as a singer.

The trip was more about socializing with the Bryans than playing golf, since I'd never studied the game nor found time to practice. They assigned me a cabin at the club named for Cliff Roberts, one of the two founders of Augusta National, along with the celebrated golfer Bobby Jones.

I don't think we discussed anything during those days that would suggest Sara Lee was stalking Hygrade. But it was clear that John Bryan, as the company's chief executive officer, was vitally interested in learning everything he could and wanted to get a measure of me, of the company, and most importantly, of Ball Park Franks.

CHAPTER 15

End of One Road, Start of Another

During the period of more than a decade that I served as Hygrade president under Hanson's ownership, the company and the meat industry had undergone a monumental transformation, bigger than any I had seen. The unprecedented pace of industry consolidation and specialization meant that meatpacking companies in order to prosper either had to be quite large, with enormous distribution networks to service the larger and larger supermarket chains—or they had to dominate a niche or category, usually by creating and reinforcing a strong brand.

Hygrade, which in the early part of the century had been a regional meatpacker, grew substantially. Still, it wasn't large enough to be among the nation's top two or three companies. But Hygrade had created something very special and valuable in its category: the Ball Park brand. The brand was initiated in the late 1950s, when the company needed a name for the hot dogs that were popular at Tiger Stadium in Detroit and were to be marketed through grocery chains. Consistent with the rising power of mass media and advertising, names like Ball Park were showing their ability to influence consumer choice, as well as to strengthen product pricing.

Consumers proved they were willing to pay a premium for what they perceived to be a more prestigious and valuable product, an awareness that was created by advertising. In our case, we told consumers again and again, in a variety of media: "They plump when you cook 'em." That clever and catchy slogan provided the rationale for a higher price. Consumers remembered it.

Some shoppers, of course, were and always would be oblivious to higher quality and were motivated by what was the cheapest price. If you were a retailer, you had to be perceived as the best and be able to charge a premium or you had to be the cheapest. Getting stuck somewhere in the middle was a losing strategy.

With constant attention to promotion, advertising, and merchandising, Ball Park Franks grew more and more in popularity, blossoming into a household name in major U.S. markets in the same way that Titleist became synonymous with golf balls and Ford with automobiles. Good fortune helped the brand as well: the razor blade hoax in 1982, for example, could have destroyed Ball Park Franks and maybe even the company. Once more, good luck was my ally, and it rubbed off on Hygrade: reports of how the company handled the crisis filled the mass media, raising consumer awareness of Ball Park Franks and our company's reputation as a responsible producer.

The company was reaping strong profits from Ball Park Franks and, to a lesser extent, from other sales and marketing strategies, much to the satisfaction of Hanson PLC. Although Newton Glekel had maintained the title as Hygrade's chairman after Hanson bought the company, his position was largely ceremonial. My reporting to Hanson executives remained direct, via the telephone.

We had spent a year or so looking for ways to grow Hygrade larger by acquisition without success. I'd even traveled to Italy to investigate the possibility of distributing hams from Parma. Then came a change in direction. The Hanson organization decided that if Hygrade wasn't able to grow by acquisition, it had better exploit its market value and be acquired by a larger company.

This change of strategy hit me like a thunderbolt. It was confirmed in a telephone call one day in late 1988 from Gordon White, senior Hanson executive for North America, a charming Englishman who spoke in a heavy accent. White informed me that Hanson intended to sell Hygrade. He assured me that the Hanson brass was very pleased with Hygrade's performance. But given that brands and branding were all the rage in consumer products, the value of the Ball Park brand seemed to be at a peak and wouldn't necessarily stay that way.

I asked how much Hanson hoped to get from a sale of the company. His answer flabbergasted me: $140 million. Thirteen years after taking Hygrade private in a transaction valued at $30 million, Hanson figured it could more than quadruple the value of its investment.

At the age of sixty-one, I knew I didn't have many more years left as a company executive. Hygrade had been the focus of my work and devotion for thirty years. I very much wanted any acquisition to proceed smoothly and advantageously for Hanson's sake, for the workers, and for me. Those thoughts quickly led me to the conclusion that Sara Lee was the likeliest and best candidate to acquire Hygrade.

I decided to make a telephone call, one of the most important of my life.

By late 1988, I had known George Bryan, Sara Lee's senior vice president of meat products, for a number of years. I also had met and talked to his older brother John, Sara Lee's chairman and chief executive. We visited once or twice in the past couple of years, including the trip to Augusta National Golf Club.

As president of a company that competed against Sara Lee and an officer of the American Meat Institute, I knew Bryan's company to be a very well run corporation with long experience and vast expertise in the meat business. Sara Lee was more than a meat conglomerate; it included a large collection of branded foods and other consumer goods. It owned Jimmy Dean pork sausages, Coach leather goods, Kiwi shoe polish, Playtex women's undergarments. and of course, Sara Lee pastries.

Had I left the sale of Hygrade up to Hanson and its advisers, there might have ensued an extended period of study and negotiation, with lots of potential buyers and an auction, as well as lawyers and investment bankers. The disposition of the company could have created several unfavorable outcomes, from my standpoint, while not necessarily improving the outcome for Hanson.

Deciding to take matters in my own hands, I called John Bryan in Chicago to let him know discreetly that Hanson was looking for a buyer. The fit would be exquisite, in my judgment, because Sara Lee already was a major and respected player in the meat industry. The conglomerate cherished and nurtured strong brands; buying Hygrade would give Sara Lee one of the hottest names in packaged foods, Ball Park Franks.

The chairman of Sara Lee, I was confident, would know exactly what to do with my tip, and I was right.

Within weeks, during a meeting in Palm Springs, I received a telephone call from John Bryan telling me the deal was done. Sara Lee had agreed to buy Hygrade from Hanson PLC.

"Our consultants told me we had to buy it," Bryan said. "And we paid too much money for it, $140 million."

Hanson evidently had stood by its guns on price, attaining exactly the amount it wanted for Hygrade. However rueful he sounded, Bryan wouldn't have paid up for the company unless he thought it was worth it.

He knew the Ball Park brand was worth its weight in gold, and he was right.

"Don't worry," he told me. "I'm not going to hold you personally responsible for financial results that justify the acquisition price." I understood from his statement that Bryan was taking the long view of the acquisition. He also was implying something else, that he expected me to stick around for a time and to lend a hand making the acquisition work.

Once the legalities were complete, Sara Lee sent an executive to run Hygrade and generously named me chairman of its processed meat division, a title without much substance or responsibility. Had I wanted or needed to stay engaged, I could have attended monthly meetings, pored over sales reports, and reviewed marketing budgets. I didn't feel comfortable in the new environment. I had gotten used to running the show around me, and I'm sure John Bryan probably presumed as much. The truth was that Sara Lee didn't really need me and was extending the courtesy of keeping me on the payroll in return for my energy, experience, and whatever wisdom I'd gained over nearly half a century.

Instead, I informed Bryan I was relinquishing my day-to-day responsibilities to his brother George, and the other meat executives, "the meatheads," as we playfully called each other. They were more than able and competent to run the operations from Sara Lee's headquarters for its meat businesses in Memphis.

My duties and obligations were almost nil. I went on two trips to pursue acquisitions for Sara Lee, neither successful. One was to try and buy Hebrew National, the maker of all-beef hot dogs in New York; the other was a run at Bar-S Foods, a maker of hot dogs based in Phoenix. Naturally, I was always available to answer questions or to advise projects.

The year that Sara Lee began to take an interest in Hygrade was also the year my wife Pat, who had been a heavy smoker for most of her adult life, experienced her first heart attack. She suffered from diabetes and other health problems, so it didn't come totally out of the blue. I can still recall the shock of the moment. She had been standing in the kitchen in our home in Howell, a restored farmhouse in farm country northwest of Detroit. She cried out in distress. I was upstairs and ran down to see what was the matter. The ambulance rushed her to our local hospital. Once she was stable, I had her transferred to the University of Michigan Medical Center.

The doctors recommended she undergo heart bypass surgery. The operation surely saved her life, though it didn't return her to good health. Pat's illness was a signal and a wakeup call, telling us both we were rapidly approaching a time in our lives when work, maintaining a home, and raising children gradually would be overtaken by the issues that face us all in our sixties: addressing our health, making sure our children are ready to lead independent lives, preparing for retirement, and considering the time we have left on this earth.

Pat and I had talked about retiring to California. I liked the place but didn't like the time zone—it was too far from friends, relatives, and acquaintances and out of phase, in terms of the time of day back east. We agreed on the idea of building a second home in the mountains of North Carolina. I bought a beautiful lot in Jefferson, overlooking the New River, a town that got its name because Thomas Jefferson had surveyed the area.

From 1989 to 1992, freed of the responsibility for Hygrade's management, I enjoyed the luxury of being able to spend, for the first time in our married life, a great deal of time with Pat at our home in Howell. We attended the fiftieth reunion of her nursing class at the Indiana University School of Nursing. We began to consider and plan our retirement in the house we were building in North Carolina. Though battling poor health, Pat supervised the construction and furnishings, taking great care to create an environment that we'd enjoy and find restful. The road trips to watch the progress at the new house were long and leisurely, giving us time to ourselves. Those were wonderful years.

In 1992, I thanked John Bryan for the opportunity to stay on at Sara Lee an additional three years following the acquisition. By that time, Sara Lee's exclusive interest in the Ball Park brand was obvious, since the company had begun dismantling Hygrade's plants and processing operations. Sara Lee owned plenty of its own slaughtering and manufacturing capacity. Closing plants wasn't cheap: it probably cost Bryan tens of millions of dollars more on top of the $140 million he paid to close Hygrade's operations. My time with the company had come to an end.

The head of Sara Lee's human resources department called one day shortly before my departure to ask if I would consider letting the company host a farewell gala in my honor. The offer was extremely gracious and generous, much in keeping with the type of class that John Bryan always had displayed.

No, I told the fellow. Instead of a party, which would cost lots of money and inconvenience a lot of people, how about you, me, and the Bryan brothers play golf and share a farewell meal together in Chicago? That's what we did.

As a departing former president, the executive most responsible for Sara Lee's acquisition of the nation's top hot dog brand, I requested one final favor: Would the company consider keeping me on the payroll, ceremonially, until December 26, 1994? On that date, exactly fifty years earlier, I was hired by the Kingan plant in Dothan as a clerk.

Was I being sentimental? Yes. My career in business had been marvelous, blessed, beyond anything I could have imagined. Half a century with the same company marked quite an achievement. I had stayed with my company through a variety of owners, through a number of name changes, and through times of prosperity, as well as adversity. I was proud of the continuity, the determination to stick to my job, to the enterprise, and to my longtime colleagues.

On my final day in the office, I gathered my things in a box, said goodbye to my secretary, and began walking toward the door.

"I hope you'll come and visit us," she said.

"No," I said, "that's not going to happen." I appreciated the sentiment. Future visits, in my opinion, would be inappropriate and disruptive. Retired executives visiting offices and plants only create distractions and disrupt operations. I vowed never to do that and kept my word.

My work-life and all my colleagues had meant the world to me. I would think of them constantly and knew I could never relive, nor would I try to recapture, a career in business that had finished for good.

CHAPTER 16

The Executive Returns to the Country

The view from our home in Michigan farm country was picturesque and tranquil. For the first time in my adult life I had time to read, to participate in the Rotary Club, and to get involved in civic and community activities that were an unthinkable luxury for a dedicated business executive.

I had time, relieved from the everyday duties of business, to reflect where I'd come from, where I'd been and what awaited me. As a child growing up in Slocomb I lived in a strictly circumscribed world, the opposite of what today would be known as "diverse." Blacks lived under strict segregation, our contacts limited and narrow. I never knew any Jews, not at school or among my parents' contemporaries. My peers in Indiana and Iowa were overwhelmingly white, members of the Catholic Church or Protestant denominations.

The ethnic mix around me changed abruptly once I arrived in Detroit in the early 1960s. Blacks, who had been plant workers, were moving into management. The city was a cluster of neighborhoods, among them Polish, Lebanese, Chaldean, and Irish. Hygrade had been founded by Sam Slotkin and was run by his son, Hugo. The Slotkins were Jewish, so I was invited to their bar mitzvahs and weddings. Sam Feig, a Jewish immigrant from the old country, taught me much about meat departments and the grocery industry. When Newton Glekel, scion of a big Jewish family in New York, arrived on the scene in 1968 as Hygrade's new chairman, he quickly took me under his wing. David Freedheim, Skip Roberts, and Leonard Epstein, all of the Jewish faith, played key roles in Hygrade's journey from meatpacking to brand management. As several of them humorously observed, for a southern farm boy I had developed quite a *Yiddishe kopf*, a Jewish way of thinking.

My annual visits to Slocomb proved to me that much had changed since my boyhood. I was thankful that much remained the same. In early 1994, during a visit to my cousins, it occurred to me that precisely a half-century had passed since my graduation from high school with the other forty-one members of my class. I called the high school, thinking a fellow class member surely must have organized a reunion, a perfectly sensible and appropriate way to mark fifty years since our graduation. No one at the school had heard of such an event.

I took the liberty of ringing Cecil Reeder, a classmate from those years. Happily, he remembered me. He thought a reunion might be possible to organize, but someone would have to volunteer to take matters in hand and do the considerable work of contacting everyone, renting a place, and planning a program.

"Call Mary Sue Hughes," he suggested; so I did.

In our high school class picture Mary Sue was captured looking downward instead of at the camera. I reminded her of that picture in our first phone conversation, so she could be sure that I indeed was her classmate.

"I've been looking down for the past fifty years," she joked. She kindly volunteered to form an organizational committee from a few classmates who still lived in the area. I agreed to be the master of ceremonies for the dinner, which was held at Highland Oaks Golf Course in Dothan.

On the appointed day, we convened once more, the Slocomb High School Class of 1944, now a group of greying senior citizens in their late sixties, having accomplished whatever we were able in our lives, having endured disappointments and rejoiced during happy times, certainly much wiser—if far less energetic—than the youngsters who came of age at the end of World War II.

Among the attendees was Helen Caldwell, whom I had known as Helen Bell before she moved to Birmingham, Alabama, got married, and raised a family. We spoke briefly about the fact that fifty years had passed since our last contact. I introduced her to my niece, Frances Bryant, who accompanied me to the event since Pat didn't feel well enough to attend.

As I walked into the building with Frances, I chatted enthusiastically— perhaps too enthusiastically—with a few classmates when Abby Phillips declared, "Clyde Riley, when you were in high school you never said anything, now you don't stop."

My life over the previous fifty years, full of experiences and personalities that defied prediction, had provided me with much to say. The evening was wonderful. We agreed to meet again soon.

Pat's health, following her heart attack and subsequent bypass surgery, was never good again. After a lifetime of smoking, she had given up cigarettes shortly before her coronary, though much damage obviously had been done and was irreversible. I was constantly fearful about the prospect of her falling grievously ill or dying.

On July 27, 2000, the event I'd been dreading transpired with shattering finality. Pat was in the kitchen making dinner for me. She asked me to change the channel for her on the television. As I left the room, she collapsed. I dialed 911 instantly, fearing in my heart that the very worst might be unfolding before me. The ambulance arrived very quickly and rushed her to our community hospital. By the time I was able to speak to a doctor about her condition, the nurses and others were acting in a manner that told me she was gone. The funeral home was called and with shocking speed and finality, a big chapter in both our lives had ended.

My daughter Margaret and my late brother's daughter, Frances, took care of the arrangements for the ceremony and burial, acts of loving kindness that I'll never forget. I worried the most about my son David, who was the closer of our two children to Pat from an emotional standpoint. Somehow, we had to get through this as a family.

For several months after Pat's death, our daughter Margaret—who, by this time was an independent woman with her own business—drove to my house from her place in Franklin, Michigan, every weekend to cook for me, so I would have meals during the week. The supermarkets were full of prepared food; I wouldn't have starved. Seeing Margaret every week helped me keep going and enhanced our already warm relationship.

I tried to keep myself busy tending to paperwork and watching over my investments. But I knew within a short time after Pat's death that much life and vitality remained. I didn't want to be alone.

A few years before Pat died, after the first reunion with classmates from Slocomb, it began to bother me that a few important events seemed erased from my memory, notably my high school graduation in 1944. My graduation from ninth grade was locked vividly in my mind, down to the white pants and blue tie I wore that day. Had something happened that day so long ago to make me want to forget? An empty space existed where I should have been able to recall standing happily in a graduation gown, receiving a diploma and rejoicing with my family.

On one of my trips south I decided on a whim to visit Helen Caldwell in Birmingham. We had gotten to know one another better after the annual reunions were initiated in 1994. Perhaps a more extensive conversation with her about the graduation—she had been the class's valedictorian—might jog a few memories from my brain. Helen and I had been on friendly terms in high school and, as strong students, were enrolled in most of the same classes and were influenced by the same teachers. We spoke a few times over the telephone. In the course of planning our reunions, Helen and Pat had become acquainted over the phone.

Helen, who had been widowed while still relatively young, couldn't have been more kind and gracious during my visit to Birmingham. We talked about the graduation, though it didn't jar any memories loose. It turned out she didn't remember much of that day either. Knowing I had been involved in business for most of my life, she arranged for us to drive over to see the Mercedes-Benz manufacturing plant nearby in Vance. We chatted and laughed about old times, our families and friends from high school.

Now that I had retired and was approaching my later years, social barriers I had felt acutely in the stratified society of rural Alabama faded away. I felt quite comfortable, for example, spending time with Helen. The Bell family was one of the most prominent in our small town. Her father ran the Segrest mercantile store, which in those days was where you could buy everything you needed from groceries to seeds to clothing. In high school, I wouldn't have dared ask Helen to spend time with me in a social setting—not that I'd ever asked any girl on a date in high school, due to my shyness and lack of access to a car. My parents were uneducated farmers, and her father was a prominent businessman. We could be classmates and friends, but certainly I would have thought it presumptuous to consider her a social peer.

Since high school, our world and the South were different from what they had been, to put it mildly: the rigid small-town distinctions of class and social status no longer mattered much for me or for my classmates. Helen had been by herself for a number of years. More recently, I had become a widower. I thought of us as friends, not separated by who our parents had been or by what rungs they had occupied in the town's pecking order. To the contrary, as adults we shared quite a bit in common, in terms of our values, which had been profoundly shaped by the place and times of our youth.

Perhaps because so much time had passed and the world looked so different from the place of our youth, I no longer felt constrained from asking Helen out socially, the barriers of fifty years earlier no longer relevant.

As a young woman, Helen had studied at the University of Alabama and was headed toward medical school when she met her future husband, Harry Caldwell. The couple married before Harry's senior year in medical school and raised four sons and a daughter. In 1972, when Helen was just forty-five, Harry fell ill with cancer and died within a few months of the diagnosis. As head of the family, she was responsible for raising her children properly, as her husband Harry would have wished. Each of the boys earned the rank of Eagle Scout. All five participated in sports, earned good grades, and assumed leadership roles in high school and college.

We began spending more time with one another, our relationship growing in warmth and mutual admiration. I had left Slocomb as a young man from a family farm, enlisted in the navy, and then pursued a business career spanning several decades in another part of the country, interacting with many types of people I'd never have met had I remained in Alabama. Was it so strange or surprising to return home and make a connection with a wonderful woman from my town, a classmate from high school?

Our children were quite accepting of our friendship, a necessary condition for continuing to see one another. Spending the rest of our lives together increasingly looked like an attractive and pleasant decision for both of us. On June, 21, 2002, we were married at Asbury United Methodist Church in Birmingham, Alabama, my son David serving as my best man and all our children in attendance.

I had grown quite attached to my residence in rural Michigan, near where most of my adult friends and associates lived. Helen had lived most of her adult life in Birmingham. She kindly and graciously agreed to come live with me in Michigan—despite the harsh winters—with the understanding that we would return to spend significant time every year in Birmingham. This compromise wasn't a difficult one to reach: our goal was to be together and to support one another, as well as our families.

Our best days have been ones that we spend quietly at home, sharing our meals, hearing from children and grandchildren. Once more, I've returned to the farm. The cares of the business world have receded, while my memories of the adventures, the cities visited, and the many fine friends and associates remain fresh and vivid. As I recall how many times individuals stepped up throughout my life and career to help me, how many times difficulties were almost magically resolved in my favor, and how long my constitution and health have remained robust, I can only conclude that a force greater than all of us made it happen, and for all the preceding I'm truly grateful.

The End

Me at age three months in front of the Rileys' farmhouse between Malvern and Slocomb, Alabama.

One of my first school pictures from Malvern Junior High School.

With my parents, Monroe and Ada Riley.

We drew water from a well during my entire childhood.

Eleventh grade. By this time I was careful with my grooming.

I'd have liked the leather jacket more if it had fit.

Waiting for the train near Great Lakes naval
base in 1946, discharge papers in hand.

My wife, Patricia Joann Thomas (1929-2000)

Our house in Howell, Michigan, built in about 1875.

The farm in Howell, Michigan.

Decisions made from my desk at headquarters were important
for Ball Park Franks and other Hygrade products.

Marcus Rothbert and I traveled together on a mission of
mercy to bring medical supplies to Moscow in 1992.

At a Detroit golf outing. The tall one at the center is Bill
Laimbeer of the Detroit Pistons. Lower right is Sam Feig, my
friend and teacher who ran Chatham's meat department.

I accepted the Silver Anvil award from the Public
Relations society in honor of Hygrade's quick and skillful
response to the hot dog tampering episode in 1982

Helen Caldwell Riley and I at her son's home in Birmingham, Alabama.

Helen and I at award ceremony honoring Skip
Roberts's service to Hospice of Michigan.

Attending the high school graduation of Helen's granddaughter.

Pat and Margaret, probably in the late 1980s or early 1990s.

Clyde and Pat Riley's son, David

Acknowledgements

First and most important is my wife, Helen. Since deciding to write this book, she and her family have encouraged and assisted me in every way possible. Nothing would have been possible without them.

David Freedheim, a talented businessman, has been a trusted friend, confidant and adviser for nearly forty years. The wife of a business associate of his advised me in the late 1970s "you have to write a book." I dismissed the idea as claptrap and forgot the conversation. About three years ago, David mentioned the idea again, which then prompted me to consider more deeply. I've got a good memory, and I'm gregarious by nature. I've met lots of people during my travels, kept documents and pictures, have stayed in touch with many of them and been surprised to hear how many of them thought my adventures in business were remarkable. They wanted to know more, as did my family. Heaven knows, I've had plenty of time during my retirement to reflect, to jot down notes and to make an orderly record of events.

As the project began to take shape, I soon realized that the turmoil in media and publishing following the Great Recession likely meant that the best and quickest course for me was to self-publish, which I did after reading an advertisement aimed at budding writers like me. My daughter Margaret, who has always been a warm and loving supporter, helped me think through, organize and write many of my thoughts and ideas on paper. David, my son, likewise was a constant source of support, warmth and companionship.

During my career, I was lucky enough to have a stalwart cadre of associates, advisers and fellow executives, several of whom played key roles at Hygrade and who functioned, when needed, as a kitchen cabinet of advisers. Bud Jarrin, who designed the Ball Park Franks package, remains a close friend. Sam Feig, an expert in big box retailing, taught me much of what I know about how consumers buy meat. I want to thank Leonard Epstein for graciously remembering and explaining Hygade's meat business in the New York area. George Bryan, member of an illustrious Mississippi family in the meat business, is and was a good friend during my career and played a major role in Hygrade's transition into the Sara Lee empire.

Skip Roberts, a lifelong advertising executive who was at W.B. Doner for most of his career, was an important actor in the creation and strengthening of the Hygrade and Ball Park Franks brands. Skip was a guide and a traveling companion; he remains a friend and the source of sage counsel. He and his wife, Carol, have helped me throughout my adult life and deserve credit for encouraging me to write this book. Gary Ridgway, who figures prominently in the Hygrade story, was and is as sharp, clear and tough-minded as any business executive can be. He was an indispensable resource.

I wish to thank my assistant Andy Laituri. He's proven to be invaluable in a hundred different ways and whenever needed. The editors and staff of Xlibris publishing, in Bloomington, Indiana, have been wonderful partners. Thank you.

Doron P. Levin, a Detroit-based journalist and author, proved to be an able, patient and skillful partner in the writing and editorial organization of this book.

Edwards Brothers Malloy
Thorofare, NJ USA
September 24, 2014